MA

**Living free**

For Phil and Rachel
who helped me to grow
in freedom and friendship


And with thanks to Sue
who typed the manuscript
and made the banner

# Living free
## Becoming the person
## God intends you to be

*Joyce Huggett*

INTER-VARSITY PRESS

**Inter-Varsity Press**
*38 De Montfort Street, Leicester LE1 7GP, England*

Unless otherwise stated, quotations from the Bible are
from the New International Version, © 1978 by the New
York International Bible Society, published in Great
Britain by Hodder and Stoughton Limited.

*First published 1984 as* Growing in Freedom
*Reprinted 1986*

**British Library Cataloguing in Publication Data**
Huggett, Joyce
  [Growing in Freedom]. Living free:
  becoming the person God intends you to be.
  1. Christian life
  I. [Growing in freedom]        II. Title
  248.4          BV4501.2
ISBN 0-85110-490-8

Typeset in Baskerville by
Parker Typesetting Service, Leicester
Printed in Great Britain by
Collins, Glasgow

*Inter-Varsity Press, is the publishing division of the Universities and
Colleges Christian Fellowship (formerly the Inter-Varsity
Fellowship), a student movement linking Christian Unions in
universities and colleges throughout the United Kingdom and the
Republic of Ireland, and a member movement of the International
Fellowship of Evangelical Students. For information about local and
national activities write to UCCF, 38 De Montfort Street, Leicester
LE1 7GP.*

# Contents

# Abbreviations

Bible references which are not taken from
the New International Version are quoted with
the following abbreviations:

| | |
|---|---|
| GNB | *Good News Bible*, 1976 |
| JB | *Jerusalem Bible*, 1966 |
| LB | *The Living Bible*, 1974 |
| Phillips | J. B. Phillips, *Letters to Young Churches*, 1958 |

# Preface

The evangelist was in full flow. 'Jesus heals broken bodies and brings people out of darkness into light. It is possible to rub shoulders with Jesus and yet remain the same person. It is also possible to touch Jesus and to be radically changed. We read of the woman with a haemorrhage in Luke 8 (40–56). She reached out and touched him and "immediately her bleeding stopped". The power of Jesus flowed into her life and she was made whole – completely new; free.'

As the preacher went on to underline these truths, my eyes met those of a young man in the congregation. The week before he had told me of his struggle against lust and sexual fantasy, a struggle which left him weary and defeated. He had been a Christian for years and had prayed for victory but nothing seemed to change. His eyes asked a question – 'If Jesus could change that woman instantly, why hasn't he done the same for me? What's wrong with me? Why was hers such a big success story while mine has "failure" written across it?'

Later that evening I talked to a Christian couple

7

whose marriage is disintegrating fast. They have been seeking help but the Lord seems to be doing little to rescue them from the pain of marital breakdown. They each need to change. God changes lives. Why doesn't he change them, then? Why doesn't he set them free from the pain of a splintering relationship?

That same evening I spoke to another Christian couple. The girl and her boy-friend told me that their relationship was being spoilt by self-indulgence. 'We know how far to go sexually. We know what is right. But we don't seem to be able to put this knowledge into practice. What's wrong with us? Why are we so in-disciplined? Why doesn't God set us free from this powerful temptation?'

The day before the evangelist's visit, my husband learnt that he was soon to have an operation. 'David in hospital? What if the operation proved unsuccessful? What if . . .?' Anxious thoughts spoilt my day. Yet Jesus said, 'Don't be anxious.' The command to 'fear not' appears in the Bible more than three hundred times. Why were my emotions so rebellious? Why was I not free to trust?

The week after the evangelist's visit, I met John. For some time he had sensed that God was calling him into full-time service but one by one the doors had closed. John grew bitter and frustrated. 'I thought I was growing as a Christian. Now I'm spiritually dry. What's more, it looks as though I'm stuck with this office job which I hate. So much for the freedom God promised me when I became a Christian. I'm not free – I'm the same person I was before I gave my life to Christ.'

We Christians know the promise, 'If the Son sets you free, you will be free indeed' (John 8:36). Most of us are

8

well acquainted with the frustration which seems to be the denial of that freedom; the kind of frustration I've just been describing. So where is the missing link? Am I the blockage to my own freedom? Will I ever taste this promised liberty? Or do I fail so consistently that God has given up on my life? Perhaps I should be satisfied with a form of Christianity which is like a thin veneer covering the old me? Or should I expect to be 'made new', set free, transformed like the early Christians seemed to be? How can I become the free person God made me to be?

These are the sort of questions we shall be examining in this book. It is not a step-by-step, ABC, do-it-yourself manual which promises freedom, maturity, wholeness, if you follow the technique. Rather it is a description of a transforming friendship; the friendship with Jesus who moves us from frustration into freedom; from immaturity into maturity.

We shall take care to observe that this freedom comes in instalments. I am persuaded that the reason so many Christians are frustrated is that they have failed to understand the true nature of freedom. You are a Christian? Then you are gloriously free. That is stage one. You don't always feel free? That is because you are in the process of becoming free. Stage two. You have yet to meet a Christian who *is* free? That is because complete freedom is not realized this side of eternity. Stage three, freedom with a capital F, is something we are all longing for. Like creation, we groan and we wait for total liberation (see Romans 8:19,23).

In the chapters that follow we look in turn at the three dimensions of freedom. We rejoice in the freedom which is ours today. We try to understand some of the methods God uses to bring us into greater freedom this side of eternity. And we anticipate, with the eye of faith, the freedom which will be ours when we meet Jesus face to face.

It is my prayer that the disillusioned in Christ may find hope in the pages of this book, that the defeated and frustrated in Christ may find a life-line to hold on to and that the disobedient may find their love for God rekindled so that the desire to obey is reborn.

The pathway to freedom is cluttered with obstacles. Let us not be foolish enough to believe that the task of removing them is easily achieved or that there is one foolproof method of doing so: healing, 'sheer gutsy obedience', a thorough working knowledge of the Bible, wrestling in prayer. These all have their place. But God is bigger than our interpretation of his methods, more compassionate than our prejudiced hearts. He has many ways of wooing us into wholeness, many ways of cheering us on, many ways of persuading us, of saying, 'Keep going. You can do it.' God has many growth-inducing schemes; plans to guide us gently into that for which we crave – ever-increasing freedom.

JOYCE HUGGETT

# 1

## *Freedom by instalments*

On the last Sunday in January I stood at the front of our church feeling unusually lost and alone. I had led the Music Group for the last time. I was about to go away for four months, a third of a year. How would I face saying good-bye to the members of the Music Group, not to mention all those other people I had grown to love? Could I get through the good-byes without embarrassing everyone by crying? How would I cope with the role-lessness of four months away from the parish?

Questions like these tumbled round my mind. Then I spotted Sue. She was pushing her way through the crowds, coming towards me. She thrust an oblong packet into my hand, whispered, 'It's for you – a kind of good-bye present', then disappeared into the crowd again, scarcely hearing my thanks.

The white tissue paper rustled in my fingers all the way home. Inside lay something soft. I unwrapped the parcel with great care and was deeply moved by what I saw. Sue had gone to a lot of trouble to make this beautiful banner. On a background of blue felt she had stitched a large black cross. At the foot of the cross lay a heap of chains, broken, powerless. Two figures stood a short distance from the chains; their faces were tilted so that they contemplated, not the chains, but the cross, the source of freedom. Their arms were raised in ecstasy. And bold yellow lettering summarized their euphoria, 'Free Indeed'.

I love that banner. It hangs in the place where I normally retreat to pray. It reminds me to give thanks for the freedom which is mine as a Christian.

But the banner also puzzled me. Those two jubilant figures stand in stark contrast to many of the Christians who come to me for counselling; a contrast, too, to my own spiritual pilgrimage so often. Many of us, it seems, are not so much free in Christ as frustrated in Christ.

I began to ask myself, 'Where is the missing link? Why are we frustrated and failing when Jesus died to secure our freedom?' Slowly the realization dawned. The concept of freedom which is often portrayed these days, total, immediate freedom, is unbiblical. The Bible nowhere suggests that freedom is a quality of life which the Christian experiences in all its fullness the moment he puts his trust in Jesus. On the contrary, the Bible encourages us to enjoy freedom in three stages. The first foretaste of this freedom *is* instant. When you put your faith in Christ you are instantly set free from the penalty of sin (see Romans 6:22).

Theologians call this dimension of freedom, 'justification'. It is the freedom which is a gift, undeserved, exhilarating, liberating. But this is not the full picture. Theologians use the word 'sanctification'[1] to describe the second dimension of freedom. It is the process by which God continues to set us free, to make us more like

Jesus. This process is gradual, often painful. It is ongoing, not finding its completion this side of the grave. The greatest freedom of all, 'glorification', the third dimension, cannot be enjoyed until the other side of eternity. The freedoms we experience on earth are just a foretaste of that greater freedom which God will grant when we meet him face to face.

But to return to my banner. Why were those two figures so jubilant? What was the freedom they were enjoying? In this chapter I propose to take a look at those questions and in later chapters to examine what I believe to be the missing link: the lack of understanding of the nature of sanctification, the gradual freedom which transforms our emotions, sexuality, attitudes, perceptions, prejudices, creativity and values. I hope to explore this facet of freedom in detail and to outline some of the methods God uses to make us into the free persons he always intended that we should become. In the last chapter we shall anticipate, all too briefly, the greatest freedom of all, glorification, heaven.

There is a hair's breadth gap between the healthy self-examination which such a study invites and unhealthy me-centredness. This book is not an invitation to Christians to navel-gaze. On the contrary, it is an encouragement to Christians who are not experiencing their full potential in Christ, and that includes most of us, to ask two questions. First, 'Lord, *how* do you want me to change to become more like you?' Second, 'Lord, how can I understand more about the mystery of your ways as you go about the task of changing me from glory to glory?' I believe that it is as we discover answers to these questions that

13

we become more open to God, more open to change, more open to become like Jesus – which is what freedom is.

## Instant freedom

How could the two figures in my banner make the extravagant claim, 'Free Indeed'? What is this instant freedom which every Christian can enjoy from the moment they turn away from the past and put their trust in Jesus?

An elderly woman put the situation well when she told me her story recently. 'I've lived a terrible life – at times I've been quite evil; done such dreadful things. Now I'm growing old and I thought to myself, "I'd love to go and live near my two beautiful grandchildren." But my daughter knows the kind of life I've led. Maybe she wouldn't want her mother so near? After all, I could influence her children, couldn't I?

'One day I told her what was going on in my mind. She's a Christian. Do you know what she said? "Why don't you put your trust in Jesus, Mummy? He can wipe out the past, set you free from it, give you a completely new start."

'At first, I hardly dared believe what she told me. But I thought it was worth a try. So I told God I was sorry for the past. I asked him to forgive me. And d'you know what happened? He forgave me. He washed me clean. He set me free from all that filth and evil. Even the guilt has gone. I didn't realize it was possible to be so happy. He's given me such joy. And I don't deserve it after what I've done.'

This simple testimony puts the situation in a nutshell. Jesus' death on the cross secured a four-fold freedom:

freedom from guilt, freedom from a sin-stained past, freedom from sin's penalty and freedom from sin's stranglehold. We must look at each of these in turn.

*Freedom from guilt*

'Even the guilt has gone', my friend claimed. How could she be so sure?

Guilt is, among other things, the skeleton which falls out of the cupboard of your memory from time to time reminding you of failure, filling you with fear. Guilt produces an inner restlessness, a lingering dread that your past misdemeanours may yet be discovered. The guilty person is at enmity with himself, with others and with God.

Take Adam, for example. When he disobeyed God, he hid from himself by blaming his wife. He used fig leaves to conceal himself from Eve. And when he heard the Lord God walking in the garden, he was full of fear and hid from him also (see Genesis 3:6–10).

The person who puts his trust in Jesus' sacrificial death is no longer at enmity with God. On the contrary, Paul reminds us of the good news: '. . . since we have been justified through faith, we *have* peace with God. . . . when we were God's enemies, we were reconciled to him through the death of his Son' (Romans 5:1, 10).

Peace with God. Friendship with God. This freedom from guilt is possible because Jesus has cancelled out the effect of our sin-stained past. As Paul delights to remind us, God himself declares us 'Not guilty!' (Romans 8:33, GNB). As we realize the truth of this reconciliation, God removes all the skeletons from the recesses of our mind and drops them into the ocean of

15

his love where they remain, not to be disturbed, not even to be brought to his remembrance again (see Hebrews 10:17).

*Freedom from the sin-stained past*
'Can this really be true? Can I really be forgiven?' The speaker was a student friend of mine who needed to share the burden of past sin with someone. He told me his story.

When he was in the sixth form at school, he slept with his girl-friend on several occasions. Against all the odds, it seemed, she became pregnant. When the child was born he was immediately adopted. But Paul carried with him the weight of the seriousness of his sin: the emotional scars he had inflicted on the girl who is now his fiancée; the responsibility of bringing an unwanted child into the world. All that was past history and he had since become a Christian. In so many ways he knew he was free; a new person. But could he ever be sure of being free from *this*?

We prayed together, asking God to give us a glimpse of what was in his Father-heart. God seemed to show Paul that the responsibility for the baby was now God's and not Paul's. He also seemed to be promising to protect the baby's mother. As for Paul himself, God seemed to apply the message of forgiveness in Luke 15 specifically to him. He seemed to see the Father running towards him, the prodigal, determined to come home at last. As we prayed, he felt the embrace of God, the enfolding of love. He wept. As the tears of repentance flowed, God seemed to show Paul what was in his Father-heart: a mixture of sorrow, unending love and tender forgiveness. Paul knew that the past was forgiven. He could now entrust his son, his fiancée and himself into the unfailing love of God, walk resolutely away from the past and go free. Undeserved? Yes. But that's what the grace of God is, 'undeserved love'. And, as the apostle reminds us in Romans 6:6, 'we know that our old self was crucified with him.'

Our former selves, our unregenerate life-style, our sinful past, our guilt: these were all pinned to the cross with Christ crucified. They have no more hold over us. The failure which once made us blush, the back-log of guilt which once weighed us down, the sin which engulfed us like the tentacles of an octopus, have no more hold over us. Their power was destroyed the moment we trusted in Jesus' saving death. Some people sense this as soon as they turn to Christ. That is why they throw up their arms in ecstasy. They are free. The weight of their guilt and their former way of life no longer burden them. These loads have been transferred to Jesus. Whether or not this truth trickles from the mind to the heart immediately, it remains a fact, to be held on to, to rejoice in.

*Freedom from the penalty of sin*
Some years ago a member of a church fellowship, Bill, was convicted of theft. He was ordered to pay a hefty fine. If he defaulted, he would be imprisoned. But Bill had no money. There was no way he could pay the fine. The night of the court case, a brown envelope dropped through his pastor's door. Inside lay a bunch of five-pound notes, the exact sum of the fine. There was also a note. 'To pay off the debt. To set my brother free.'

God warned Adam that disobedience would result in death. Paul reminds us that the wages of sin is death

(Romans 6:23). The reason why Christians rejoice is that Jesus' crucifixion rescued them from the death penalty which was the inevitable consequence of their sinful past. Because Jesus died, we are set free from sin and its penalty.

Like Bill, there was no way we could pay the debt ourselves. So God allowed Jesus 'to be made sin' for us sinners. The judgment which should have been heaped on us, fell on him. Thus a transference took place. Jesus took my sin and paid the full debt of it by suffering a cruel, physical, criminal's death. His death secured my freedom.

When Jesus hung, tortured, dying, on Calvary's cross, he uttered the words, 'It is finished.'

Finished! Accomplished! This is legal language. The word was often written across bills in those days. It means, 'Paid!' 'Transaction completed!' 'Score settled!'

We were powerless to settle the score for ourselves, to share in the act of sin-bearing. But when, through faith, we surrendered our lives to God, God shifted the blame and responsibility of our wrong-doing on to the shoulders of Jesus. In God's sight, it was as though, when Jesus died, we had died with him. God now looks on us as though we had never sinned.

Our debt has been cancelled. Paid. We are free from the penalty of sin. God has forgiven us.

When God forgives, he does not play a game of 'Let's pretend': 'Let's pretend they never sinned.' No. He sees us as we are: soiled, helpless, innately sinful. He knows what he is taking on when he promises to love us. Even so, he applies the righteousness of Jesus to us. He not only puts us right with himself; when he looks on us he sees, not the sin-stained me, but his pure and holy Son.

18

It is as though I have been clothed with the unsoiled garment of Jesus' life of obedience.

This is a mystery. It can never be fully understood, fully explained. To put it in words is rather like trying to describe a sunset to a man born blind or a symphony to a man born deaf.

But the Christian who knows in his heart that he has put his faith in Jesus' death can be lost in wonder, love and praise. He has been set free (Romans 6:22). This freedom is instant. Irreversible. Complete. The penalty has been paid. God will not go back on this act. The deed is done.

*Freedom from sin's bondage*
Everyone who walks this earth has sinned. Ever since the fall, man has been enslaved by sin. Body, mind, emotions were shot through with evil. Sin has been the dominant factor in our lives. Ruth Burrows puts it well, 'Sin is to be seen as an orientation, a more or less continual series of choices against what one knows in one's deepest heart is right.'[2] Our orientation has been against God, not for him. As God himself observed, even our thoughts, inclinations and imaginations are evil (see Genesis 6:5). Paul expresses it in strong language, 'You used to be slaves to sin' (Romans 6:17).

A slave is a person who is owned by another; someone without rights who can be used, abused and disposed of in any way the owner chooses. A slave is compelled to obey his master. He has no right or power to say 'No'.

Paul is saying, 'Once you were slaves of sin. Sin was your master, and you were forced to do all the evil things that sin ordered you to do; you had no power to say "No". But now you have died so far as your relation

19

to sin is concerned, and you need pay no more heed to the dictates of sin. Or, to put it another way, a slave's former owner has no more authority over him if he becomes someone else's property. That is what has happened to you. You have passed from the service of sin into the service of God.'[3]

I look at my banner. I read the words, 'Free Indeed'. And I drink in the implications. I am now free to say 'No' when sin and temptation lurk in the shadows of my life.

In Galatians 4:3, 8, Paul uses even stronger language, 'We too were slaves of the ruling spirits of the universe . . . slaves of beings who are not gods' (GNB). Many Christians understand all too well the situation Paul is describing here. In the past, sinful acts became obsessional. Lust, selfishness, dabbling in fringe occult activities, seemed to possess a compulsive, magnetic power.

The moment you placed your trust in Jesus, that power was broken. This does not mean you cannot be attracted by sin any more, as we go on to consider later in this chapter. It does mean that the chains which held you captive, the powers which once forced you into sinful habit patterns, have no more hold over you. Jesus has destroyed their stranglehold. As Paul proclaimed, 'It is for freedom that Christ has set us free' (Galatians 5:1).

How, when we were condemned to die, did Jesus grant us release? What was the cost to himself?

## The cost of freedom

Archbishop Anthony Bloom tells a story which reminds

us that our freedom was bought at a cost. The story is of Natalie, a Russian woman of whom little is known except her name and the fact that she lived in Russia in the year 1919, when civil war ravaged that country.

As the war swept over Russia like a terrifying storm, city after city fell prey to one army after another. In one city, a young mother, the wife of an officer in the White Army, found herself trapped because this city had fallen into the hands of the Red Army. If they discovered her, she and her children would be killed instantly. What could she do to preserve their lives?

On the outskirts of the city, she discovered a small, wooden cabin. She would hide there until the first surges of conflict were over. Then she would escape.

Towards evening on her second day in hiding, someone knocked at her door. She opened it in fear, and stood face to face with a young woman of her own age. The woman spoke in whispers. Her message was urgent.

'You must flee at once. You've been discovered. Tonight the soldiers will come. You are to be shot.'

The mother looked down at her two small children. Escape? How could she escape? Her children were too young to walk far. They would be recognized at once. The plan was unthinkable. She must prepare to die.

But the woman, Natalie, persisted.

'Don't worry about the children. I'll stay here. They won't even look for you.'

'You stay here? But they'll kill you.'

'Yes. But I have no children.'

That night Natalie came back. The mother and her two small boys escaped into the woods. Natalie faced the soldiers – alone. Natalie faced death – another woman's death – alone.

At any moment, Natalie could have stepped out of the wooden cabin. At any moment she could have become Natalie again. At any moment she could have stepped into freedom. She made her choice: to stay inside the cabin.

Hours passed. With the cold of morning they came. The door was brutally battered open and, without bothering to drag her outside, they shot her where she was. Friends found her later that day – in bed. Dead.

Almost 2,000 years before, a young man of Natalie's age waited for his death. His name was Jesus. He died in my place. But the price of my release was more even than his life.

When he died, Jesus, the spotless Son of God, took upon himself all the guilt and horror of my sin. He suffered the whole weight of the judgment that was due to me. He experienced 'the aweful tearing apart of fellowship between the Father and the Son'[1] which made him cry on the cross 'My God, my God, why have you forsaken me?' (Mark 15:34). That was the price he paid to secure my freedom: freedom from guilt, freedom from my sin-stained past, freedom from the penalty of sin, freedom from sin's enslavement. Now I can say with David and with Paul,

> Happy are those whose wrongs are forgiven,
>     whose sins are pardoned!
> Happy is the person whose sins the Lord
>     will not keep account of!
> (Psalm 32:1–2, quoted in Romans 4:7–8, GNB).

Now I know what it means to be 'Free Indeed'.

# Notes for chapter one

[1] For a fuller discussion of justification and sanctification, see Bruce Milne, *Know the Truth* (Inter-Varsity Press, 1982), chapters 4 and 5.

[2] Ruth Burrows, *Before the Living God* (Sheed and Ward, 1975), p. 11.

[3] F. F. Bruce, *Romans, Tyndale New Testament Commentaries* (Inter-Varsity Press, 1963), p. 140.

[4] David Atkinson, *Wings of Refuge* (Inter-Varsity Press, 1983), p. 53.

# 2

# *Freedom in the overlap*

Louise is one of those people who can tell you the day and the time when she opened her life to Christ; the exact place where she tasted her first sip of the freedom we discussed in chapter one. 'It was a fantastic experience. I knew I was forgiven. I knew God had given me his Spirit. I felt a new and different person.'

Unfortunately, no-one helped Louise to understand what freedom in Christ is and what it is not. When she came to see me three years after her conversion, she felt an abysmal failure. 'I really thought that Jesus had given me a completely new life – his life; that I wouldn't be tempted any more, that I was dead to sin, therefore couldn't sin again. Then I met Steve. He's not a Christian but I fell in love with him. He wanted us to sleep together, so we did. I enjoyed it. I didn't realize it was wrong. But now I've come to see that I'm a hopeless failure. Can God ever forgive me and set me free again?'

My heart went out to Louise. Why hadn't anyone taught her that although Jesus had set her free from her sinful past, she was not hermetically sealed against sin for ever? She was not free from the subtle wiles of Satan, she was not free from temptation's apparent attractions, she was not dead to the desires of the flesh or the old nature. Neither was she free from pain, struggle and the responsibility to make God-choices.

You may not have experienced a crisis conversion as Louise did. Not all Christians do. Some grow into the realization that Jesus' death is the open door through which we pass to attain fellowship, union, with God, salvation. Whether yours was an instant conversion or a prolonged one, there are certain facts you should know about your present position in Christ if you are not to fall into the kind of trap which caught Louise unawares; if you are to reach your full potential as a Christian.

When you put your faith in Christ, it is true to say that you were translated from the kingdom of darkness into the kingdom of light. It is true to say that you moved from death to life. It is true to say that you, who were once a slave to sin and an enemy of God, became his friend, instantly. These are all Bible truths. They cannot be contradicted. (See Romans 5:10; 6:12.) But when you put your trust in God's way of salvation, you did not leap over the cross which bridges the gap between sinful man and the inaccessible God, straight into God's glorious presence where sin ceases to exist. Neither were you ejected straight from the kingdom of darkness into the new Jerusalem, the world of sinlessness.

The cross of Christ penetrated the prison walls which held you captive in the kingdom of darkness. The cross of Christ gave you access to God's kingdom. But the journey has only just begun. One day Jesus will take you on the next stage of that journey. Then he will lead you into his Father's glorious presence, the new heaven and

25

the new earth; the new Jerusalem. Meanwhile there is a great deal of learning to do. Meanwhile you live your life in the now: 'The overlap' (to borrow Jean Darnall's phrase[1]), the place where the old is restored, the old is renewed, the old is transformed, preparing us for the 'new'.

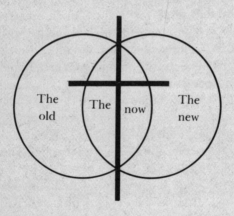

You have turned your back on the old life; walked away from it. You have walked, by way of Christ's cross, towards that stage of the journey where all things will be, not only new, but perfect. You are a pilgrim, travelling. You are a pupil, learning. You are a child of the world, being changed so that you can take your place in the kingdom of God.

What is the overlap? What kind of freedom does the Christian enjoy there? What is the purpose of this in-between existence? These, and allied questions, are the themes which will occupy most of this book. In discovering the answers to them we discover the secret of our identity, the purpose for our lives, and we journey deeper and deeper into God's freedom.

## What is the overlap?

What does the Bible say about the overlap, this middle world? The Bible nowhere uses the term. It does describe the concept.

Take Jesus' teaching about his kingdom, for example. The kingdom of God is a here and now kingdom. 'The kingdom of God is within you' (Luke 17:21). 'Yours is the kingdom of God' (Luke 6:20). But the kingdom is also future. 'I will not drink again of the fruit of the vine until the kingdom of God comes' (Luke 22:18). Jesus is not contradicting himself. He is describing the overlap. The kingdom is here. It is also coming. This is a mystery. A paradox.

## The overlap: a place of fellowship with God

The overlap is the place where we grow in trust, in Christlikeness and in freedom. It is also the place where we grow in our awareness of God. In a recent radio programme, 'Prayer and Meditation', people of all religious persuasions were invited to describe their attempts at achieving union with God. The programme pin-pointed an eternal truth – man is hungry for God. He will sacrifice time, energy, food, sleep, to experience fellowship with the Almighty. As St Augustine put it, 'Thou hast made us for Thyself, and our hearts will know no rest until they rest in Thee.'

The Bible assures us that the moment we turn to Christ, we have fellowship with God. We become his

27

friends: '. . . he made us his friends through the death of his Son' (Romans 5:10, GNB).

The overlap is the place where this friendship grows and deepens through prayer, Bible reading and fellowship with other Christians.

But, precious as this relationship with God is, it is incomplete this side of eternity. This is not a cause for despondency but for excitement. Now there is an inequality in our intimacy with God: rather like the relationship between a foetus and the mother. But the day is coming when we shall see God face to face. The friendship we shall enjoy with him then will be even deeper and richer than those moments here on earth when we experience a foretaste of that union.

Paul puts it powerfully in 1 Corinthians 13:12, 'Now we see but a poor reflection; then we shall see face to face. Now I know in part; then I shall know fully, even as I am fully known.'

Does it sometimes seem as though your prayers do not penetrate the ceiling, let alone the ears of Christ? Does the Bible sometimes seem a dry and dusty tome rather than a living letter from God? Do you sometimes despair of experiencing oneness with Christ? Take heart. This frustration is an inevitable consequence of living in the overlap; of seeing God through a cracked and tarnished mirror. The day *is* coming when we shall see him face to face and talk to him face to face and even be like him.

## The overlap: a place where God transforms us

As we shall go on to observe in detail, the overlap is the place where God begins to effect this transformation;

where we begin to live a new life. Symbolically we died with Christ. Now we have been raised from death into life; resurrected. The overlap is the place where we enjoy this resurrection, where we begin to enjoy the resources of the heavenly life: peace with God, God's undeserved love, eventual victory. As Paul expresses it, 'Therefore, if anyone is in Christ, he is a new creation; the old has gone, the new has come' (2 Corinthians 5:17).

The new *has* come. But this is not a definitive statement. Paul has already made this clear in his first letter to the Corinthian Christians. The new creation they are privileged to enjoy in the here and now is simply a foretaste of a resurrection much more glorious than man's mind can begin to conceive. 'Listen, I tell you a mystery: We will not all sleep, but we will all be changed – in a flash, in the twinkling of an eye, at the last trumpet. For the trumpet will sound, the dead will be raised imperishable, and we will be changed. For the perishable must clothe itself with the imperishable, and the mortal with immortality . . .' (1 Corinthians 15:51–53). On that day, we shall 'bear the likeness of the man from heaven' (1 Corinthians 15:49).

The overlap is the middle-world where we mortals are treated to the freedom Christ delights to give. But this freedom is but a pale reflection of the immortal freedom we shall enjoy when he returns.


## The overlap: a place of hope

This makes our middle-world existence a stage of hope. Hope in the Christian sense does not mean a vain longing. It means certainty. We do not hope for something we already possess. We anticipate it with eagerness, longing and gratitude. This hope should characterize our days as we wait in the overlap. It is the hope which throbs through most of the negro spirituals. 'This world is not my home, I'm just a-passing through.'

That is correct. This world as we experience it today is not home. We are en route for the Promised Land. The Bible makes this quite clear. 'The creation waits in eager expectation . . . the whole creation has been groaning as in the pains of childbirth' (Romans 8:19,22). Why? Creation, and we are a part of that world, is held in tension, the world of not yet. Creation has seen the King, it has received a foretaste of the freedom which will one day be complete; it therefore agonizes as it waits for the King's return, when God's freedom will be absolute. That freedom is coming. But we live in the 'not yet'.

But this hope is not empty and futile. It is life-giving.


## The overlap: a place of difficulty, tension, struggle, choice

Even so, the 'not yet', the overlap, is inevitably a place of difficulty, struggle, tension, doubt, of 'groaning'. The overlap is the kingdom of the in-between. I have easy access to my past: old habits, powerful emotions, persuasive longings. I also have access to the Father's throne. And I have access to my inner longings: the desire to gratify self, fulfil self and promote self. Thus the overlap becomes a battle-ground.

Jesus has become the Lord of my life, my King. He has de-throned self's despotism. At least, that is the theory. That is the goal. But I have held the reins for a very long time. I don't abdicate ownership that easily. And often Jesus and I reach deadlock.

Satan doesn't let go of his own without a struggle either. Yes, Jesus has conquered Satan. Satan is the defeated foe. Defeated, but not ineffective. And very active.

We must understand this warfare if we are to survive life in the overlap. The triumphalistic teaching which claims, 'Turn to Jesus and everything in the garden will be rosy', is unbiblical. Listen to the warnings Jesus gave. 'If anyone would come after me, he must deny himself' (Luke 9:23); 'I did not come to bring peace, but a sword' (Matthew 10:34); 'Can you drink the cup I drink or be baptised with the baptism I am baptised with?' (Mark 10:38) (overwhelmed with sorrow and pain).

Christianity, an easy life? That is not Jesus' definition. He foretells indescribable pain and problems: self-denial, division and turmoil. When you become a Christian your problems do not disappear overnight. You exchange one set of problems for another. The difference is that, whereas once you were expected to handle your problems alone, now the Lord is there shielding you from danger, giving you victory, pouring in courage (see Psalm 3:3).

### The overlap: a place of choosing

One reason why the overlap presents the Christian with conflict rather than peace is that the overlap is a place where adult choices must be made.

We saw in the last chapter that there was a time when we were in bondage to sin, enslaved by it. We had no alternative but to pull in a God-less direction. That is no longer the case. Now that Jesus has cut us loose from the chains which held us, we are faced with a series of choices which sometimes seem to tear us limb from limb. The choice, so often, is between what I want, what I would have done in the past, and what God wants, what I know to be appropriate behaviour now that I am a child of God. And Satan makes sure that God's way appears dull and boring; that the path of sin is dazzling in its beauty. He's been playing this trick since Genesis 3.

The Bible acknowledges this struggle. Paul understood the full force of it. 'I do not understand what I do. For what I want to do I do not do, but what I hate I do. . . . So I find this law at work: When I want to do good, evil is right there with me. . . . What a wretched man I am! Who will rescue me from this body of death?' (Romans 7:15–24).

Frustrated in Christ? Struggling in the overlap? You are in good company. The overlap is the place where we must keep striving, as Paul did. (See Philippians 2:12–13.) And as the writer to the Hebrews reminds us, 'Consider him who endured such opposition from sinful men, so that you will not grow weary and lose heart. In your struggle against sin, you have not yet resisted to the point of shedding your blood' (Hebrews 12:3–4).


### The overlap: the place where we are refined

Peter helps us to understand why life in the overlap is often fraught with frustration, pain and difficulty. 'Their purpose is to prove that your faith is genuine' (1 Peter 1:7, GNB).

If that sounds like a cruel way of proving your integrity, read on. 'Even gold, which can be destroyed, is tested by fire; and so your faith, which is much more precious than gold, must also be tested, so that it may endure. Then you will receive praise and glory and honour on the Day when Jesus Christ is revealed' (1 Peter 1:7, GNB).

The reason why the going is tough in the overlap is because it is your apprenticeship, your training-ground, your preparation for the glorious future which God has guaranteed will be yours (see Romans 8:31–39).

The overlap is the place where you are being refined so that on the day when Jesus returns you will have been so changed into his likeness that you are ready to take your place as part of the bride of Christ. This makes the overlap a place of privilege. Awesome. It assures us that our glorification is guaranteed (see Romans 8:30ff.).

## The overlap: the first instalment

How can we be sure that God will not give up on us; that he will so transform us into his likeness that we are ready to be presented mature in him when he returns? Paul assures us that our eventual glorification is guaranteed. 'Since we have now been justified by his blood, how much more shall we be saved from God's wrath through him! For if, when we were God's enemies, we were reconciled to him through the death of his Son, how much more, having been reconciled, shall we be saved through his life!' (Romans 5:9).

Commenting on this passage, John Stott observes:

What the apostle means is surely this, that our

33

developing, ripening Christian character is evidence that God is at work upon us and within us. The fact that God is thus at work in our lives gives us confidence that He is not going to give up the job uncompleted. If He is working in us now to transform our character, He is surely going to bring us safely to glory in the end.. . .

There is a strong presumption that we shall never be allowed to fall by the way, but shall be preserved to the end and glorified. This is not just sentimental optimism; it is grounded upon irresistible logic. The logic of it is this, that if, when we were enemies, God reconciled us through giving His Son to die for us, how much more, now we are God's friends, will He finally save us from His wrath by His Son's life? If God performed the more costly service (involving His Son's death) for His enemies, He will surely perform the less costly service now that His erstwhile enemies are His friends. Meditate on this until you see the irrefutable logic of Paul's argument.[2]

## The overlap: the guarantee of a greater freedom

God is not going to give up the job uncompleted. A charming children's story illustrates this soul-satisfying truth. The heroine of the parable is Yellow, a caterpillar who often dreamed of greater freedom but whose concept of the world of flight and butterflies was blurred and confused.

One day, when, as usual, thoughts of butterflies were occupying her caterpillar-brain, she came across a curious sight: a grey-haired caterpillar hanging upside-down on a branch. Seeing that he was caught in some hairy stuff, Yellow offered her assistance.

'You seem in trouble, can I help?'

'No, my dear, I have to do this to become a butterfly.'

A butterfly! Yellow's caterpillar-heart leapt. Could this be her great opportunity?

'Tell me, sir, what is a butterfly?'

'It's what you are meant to become. It flies with beautiful wings and joins the earth to heaven... .'

Yellow's heart somersaulted in hope. 'Me! A butterfly? It can't be true! How can I believe there's a butterfly inside you and me, when all I see is a fuzzy worm? How does one become a butterfly?' she added, pensively.

'You must want to fly so much that you are willing to give up being a caterpillar.'

'You mean to die?' asked Yellow.

'Yes and no,' he answered. 'What *looks* like you will die but what's *really* you will still live. Life is changed, not taken away. Isn't that different from those who die without ever becoming butterflies?'

'And if I decide to become a butterfly,' said Yellow hesitantly, 'what do I do?'

'Watch me. I'm making a cocoon. It looks like I'm hiding, I know, but a cocoon is no escape. It's an in-between house where the change takes place. It's a big step, since you can never return to caterpillar life. During the change, it will seem to you or anyone who might peep that nothing is happening – but the butterfly is already becoming. It just takes time!'

Yellow was torn with anguish. What if she became this thing called butterfly and her friends failed to recognize this new self? At least she knew that caterpillars can crawl and eat and love in a limited way. What happens if a caterpillar gets stuck in a cocoon? Could she risk losing the only life she had known when it seemed so unlikely she could ever become a glorious winged creature? All she had to go on was a caterpillar who believed sufficiently to take the leap of faith. And hope.

The grey-haired caterpillar continued to cover himself with silky threads. As he wove the last bit around his head he called:

'You'll be a beautiful butterfly – we're all waiting for you!'

And Yellow decided to take the risk also.

For courage she hung right beside the cocoon and began to spin her own.

'Imagine, I didn't even know I could do this. That's some encouragement that I'm on the right track. If I have inside me the stuff to make cocoons – maybe the stuff of butterflies is there too.'

And, of course, the stuff of butterflies *was* there. Yellow eventually emerged 'a brilliant, yellow, winged creature – a wonderful sight!'[3]

There will be times during life in the overlap when you are assailed with similar doubts, when you ask with Yellow: 'How can I believe there's a butterfly inside me when all I see is a fuzzy worm?' Or, to put it another way, 'How can I believe God's Spirit dwells within me when all I see is a despicable failure?'

There will be times when life in the overlap will seem dull, drab, constricted; when you seem to be stripped of freedom rather than liberated.

And there will be times when you seriously question whether the risk was worth taking; whether you have died to the past for no purpose.

But God is Lord of the overlap. Even when your life seems of little value, even when you detect no spiritual movement, changes *are* taking place; the kind of changes which split open cocoons and produce butterflies. God is changing you. He has guaranteed to make you perfect in the end. He has guaranteed to make you free.

## Notes for chapter two

[1] Jean Darnall, *Life in the Overlap* (Lakeland, 1977).
[2] John Stott, *Men Made New* (Inter-Varsity Press, 1966), pp.15,20.
[3] Trina Paulus, *Hope for the Flowers* (Paulist Press, 1972).

# 3

# *The truth shall set you free*

One of the biggest barriers to freedom and wholeness is worldliness. By worldliness, I do not mean indulging in cinema-going, dancing or alcohol. By worldliness, I mean the subtle infiltration of human philosophies, values and attitudes which we all imbibe, sometimes without realizing it. These worldly philosophies come in various disguises. They seem attractive, rational and plausible; sometimes their voice is so persuasive we wonder why we have failed to view the Christian life from this perspective in the past. These seemingly reasonable philosophies eventually control us, corner us and so govern our behaviour that we lose our freedom, or never fully realize our potential in Christ.

Let me give some illustrations of what I mean.

## Freedom lost

When I was in Singapore, I met a young man, Gee Ming, who told me his story of freedom lost.

Gee Ming used to lead the Youth Group of the church

he attended. He loved the young people and they responded to his leadership well. But Gee Ming, a new convert, was a young man with heavy financial commitments. Over a period of time, unknown to anyone in the church, he got into serious debt. He was ashamed of this predicament; afraid to discuss it with his Pastor or the Elders of the church. Instead, he fell back into his pre-Christian life-style: gambling, speculating, embezzlement, even overt theft. He knew that these shady practices were squeezing him back into the world's mould but the pull of the world proved stronger than his commitment to Christ. A voice inside him would whisper, 'It will only be for a short while, then you can live as a Christian again.' This persuasive voice sounded so sensible in the circumstances, but by the time I met him, he had lost the joy in Christ he had once enjoyed. Moreover, he had withdrawn from the fellowship, resigned from church leadership and actively avoided any encounter with his former Christian friends. 'It's over now. I miss it all terribly – the church, I mean. They were my family. It's left a big hole in my life and I don't know how to fill it.'

Or I think of a student who came to see me recently. He described his friendship with another male student on campus. He talked about the tangled emotions inside him and then described their homosexual activity. We looked together at what the Bible says about homosexuality, whereupon he rebelled. 'It's so unfair. The church has explained away divorce. Some Christians even manage to disregard the Bible's teaching on promiscuity. In twenty years time they will have changed their views on homosexual behaviour. I'm just unlucky. Why should I be stuck with the Bible's rigid teaching on the subject? It makes me really angry with God.'

This approach to God, the pride and rebellion which results in a Christian adjusting God's instructions to his life-style rather than adjusting his life-style to God's revealed word, is not new. This was Adam's sin in Genesis 3. It crops up today with monotonous regularity. Fall into this trap, and you not only lose sight of the truth, you wave goodbye to freedom also.

Of course, not all Christians approach the Bible with this warped viewpoint: 'If this is what the Bible says and it doesn't suit me, I can argue it away.' Some find themselves squeezed into a world-shaped mould because of ignorance of God's word or an inability to apply it to the crevices, the nooks and crannies of their life. So a research student uses the department's photo-copier without recording what he owes: 'Everybody does.' The young professional arrives late for work or leaves early: 'Everybody does.' A sixth-former removes stationery from school for personal use or for Sunday School purposes: 'Everybody does it.' A girl sleeps with her boy-friend: 'Everybody does. It's old-fashioned not to.'

Cultural norm, not the Bible, has become the ruling principle of the age even for some Christians. It is one of today's tragedies. The cultural norm has bewitched Christians, blinding them to the truth, lulling them into a false sense of security. The resulting complacency is a curse and freedom's thief.

And if Satan fails to ensnare us through the sweet reasonableness of worldly attitudes, pride or cultural conditioning, he may sidle up to us, snake-like, with another attractive proposition. 'The thing that counts in your relationship with God is feelings: warm, loving feelings, ecstatic feelings, emotional experiences.' Some of us are gullible enough to fall for this. When singing worship choruses we find our hearts strangely warmed and think we mean it when we sing, 'Father, we love you, we worship and adore you . . .'. But as the feeling of warmth evaporates, our freedom goes with it unless we understand that freedom has nothing to do with feelings; it has much to do with obedience.

## The source of freedom

Jesus, the man who encountered identical pressures, the God-made-man who blazed the trail, rejecting all philosophies and ways forward which were at variance with the Father's will, the one who showed us how to cast off the clutter of cultural conditioning and the expectations of others, speaks incisively into these situations. With one powerful, economical sentence, he points the way to freedom and to its source: 'If you obey my teaching . . . you will know the truth, and the truth will set you free' (John 8:31–32, GNB).

There are two key phrases in this sentence: 'If you obey my teaching . . .' and 'the truth will set you free'. One phrase, 'the truth will set you free' receives much attention these days. It is the focus of many sermons. But the qualifying clause, 'If you obey . . .' is not given such prominence. Yet truth without obedience does not equal freedom. No. The equation is this: *truth + obedience = freedom*.

Some of us are all too like the young man who confessed to me recently, 'I listened carefully to the sermon in church last night. It was a terrific sermon. But as soon as I walked through the church door, I forgot its teaching and deliberately sinned.' When we behave like this, we reject the freedom God offers. I once saw a child who had failed to grow normally because she could not absorb food into her system. It passed through her body without nourishing it. We must avoid a similar situation in our spiritual growth through refusing to allow God's spiritual nourishment to take its full effect.

Rather, we must be imitators of Christ, who, in the agony of Gethsemane and the anguish of the wilderness, kept the cup of the Father's will before him and drank it even when the taste was bitter.

The theme of obedience, like a recurring theme in a piece of music, runs through the entire Bible: 'Today, if you hear his voice, do not harden your hearts . . .' (Psalm 95:7–8); 'Why do you call me, "Lord, Lord," and do not do what I say?' (Luke 6:46); 'Do whatever he tells you' (John 2:5).

The Psalmist saw how obedience and the truth were inter-related. Obedience to the truth results in wisdom, insight and discernment: 'I have more understanding than the elders, for I obey your precepts' (Psalm 119:100). Obedience to the truth results in objective living: 'How can a young man keep his way pure?' Not by trusting feelings or caving in to their clamouring demands, but, 'By living according to your word' (Psalm 119:9). Obedience to the truth is the prerequisite for realistic goal-setting: 'Your word is a lamp to my feet' (Psalm 119:105). In short, obedience to the truth provides the man of God with a purpose in life; obedience is the secret of full and joyous living. 'I will live in perfect freedom, because I try to obey your teachings' (Psalm 119:45, GNB).

In his book, *Guru Jesus*, Robert Van de Weyer

similarly testifies to the life-changing power of obedience. The author, an English public school boy, became a drop-out, rejecting traditional standards and
Christianity. He made an overland journey to India
where he tried in vain to find a satisfactory Guru and
attempted to adopt the life-style of a wandering ascetic.
Finally, he settled in a Christian community where he
decided to try an experiment. He would make Jesus his
Guru for a test period of six months. 'During this time
I shall act as a full disciple studying his teachings
closely and following them as far as I can, regardless of
whether I fully understand or agree with them.'[1]
Within weeks of obeying the truth revealed in the
Word of God, this is what he wrote, 'I hardly think I
need wait the full six months. I am already firmly
nailed to the cross of Jesus and am enjoying it enor-
mously.'[2]

Obedience is the source of freedom.


## The truth

If we would be free, we, too, must obey the truth. But
what is this elusive thing called truth? Where do we
find it? How does it release us?

In Hebrew thought the truth was that which holds
water; that which does not give way or collapse; what is
real, correct, a sound basis for conduct. The Bible
encourages us to believe that this truth is revealed in
three ways. The truth is a person: Jesus. The truth is
God's teaching: the written Word of God contained in
the Bible. The truth is God's word applied to our
individual situation by the enlightenment of the Holy
Spirit: God's will obeyed.

Paul puts this powerfully in his letter to the Colossians. 'Make sure that no one traps you and deprives you of your freedom by some secondhand, empty, rational philosophy based on the principles of this world instead of on Christ' (Colossians 2:8, JB). 'You must live your whole life according to the Christ you have received – Jesus the Lord; you must be rooted in him and built on him and held firm by the faith you have been taught, and full of thanksgiving' (Colossians 2:6–7, JB).

If we would safeguard our freedom, then three things are required of us: to live biblically, to be Jesus-centred and to be obedient. I have stressed the need to be obedient and we return to this again in a later chapter. We must now look at the other two emphases.

## Living biblically

While I have been writing this book, two Psalms have burned their message into my heart in a new way: Psalm 19 and Psalm 119. These paeons of praise are the Psalmist's personal testimony, expressing what God's Word meant to him, what God's Word did for him, what God's Word is. When the Christian approaches God's written Word with similar attitudes: humility, teachableness, receptivity, he strides through frustrations into freedom just as the Psalmist seems to have done – not painlessly, but effectively.

### An attitude to God's Word
As I started to read Psalm 119, I found myself swept along in its current, like a little stick bobbing along in the waters of a laughing mountain stream. I had to remind myself that the poet was a king, a man who, humanly

44

speaking, had arrived, reached the top. Yet he delighted in God's Word (16, 162), treasured it (11), steeped himself in it (15, 27, 48), respected it (2, 115, 129), recited it (13), remembered it (52), pored over it (97, 99, 148), examined it (94), and determined never to veer from it (110, 157). C. S. Lewis sums up the Psalmist's attitude, 'The Order of the Divine mind, embodied in the Divine Law, is beautiful. What should a man do but try to reproduce it, so far as possible, in his daily life? His "delight" is in those statutes (16); to study them is like finding treasure (14); they affect him like music, are his "songs" (54); they taste like honey (103); they are better than silver and gold (72). As one's eyes are more and more opened, one sees more and more in them, and it excites wonder (18). This is not priggery nor even scrupulosity; it is the language of a man ravished by a moral beauty. If we cannot at all share his experience, we shall be the losers.'[3]

*What God's Word does*

We must not only identify with, take on board, the Psalmist's attitude to the revealed, written Word of God, we must be equally assured of its effectiveness. There is space here to select only a few of the poet's thoughts: God's Word is life-giving (119:50; 19:7), life-preserving (119:92), life-transforming (19:11). It is perfect, trustworthy, upright, clear and true (19:7).

God's Word revives (119:25, 107), restores and liberates. It makes one wise (119:98; 19:7), keeps one from evil (119:101), gives hope to the helpless (119:114), light in the darkness (119:130), guidance in perplexity (119:105).

If all these things are true, they show us how to live

45

biblically and how to approach the discipline of Bible reading. The kernel is this: steep yourself in the Bible, examine it, meditate on it, obey it. We shall take these one at a time.

*Steep yourself in it*

In the summer of 1983, I had the privilege of ministering to Christians in Singapore and Malaysia. These first-generation Asian Christians knew what it meant to steep themselves in the Word of God. They were hungry for it, like refugees queuing for food. You could not give them enough. They enjoyed the Word of God, explored it, were excited by it.

How can we over-privileged, over-fed Christians in the West rekindle our enthusiasm for God's Word? One way, I believe, is to break free from the man-made or self-imposed straitjacket so many of us strap round ourselves whenever we take God's Word into our hands: the 'this-is-the-way-to-do-it' approach.

God's Word, the Bible, as Augustine once described it, is 'our letter from home'. It is also the yardstick of our lives, containing guidelines for our conduct. The Bible is a treasury: promise after promise from God to the believer. There is no one, fixed, approved way to read this library from God, but many ways. And we must not only steep ourselves in it, but learn to enjoy it.

We learn to enjoy it by reading it. Read it often. Read it daily. Read it right through. Sometimes start at Genesis and work your way through to Revelation, perhaps with a single aim in mind, like underlining every command you find or placing a mark against specific promises. At other times, take a book or one of the epistles. Read it through at one sitting. Then enjoy the

Psalms. Allow yourself to be caught up in their infectious praise. And sometimes work your way through a book slowly, paragraph by paragraph.

Expect God to speak to you in a variety of ways as you read. Sometimes he does this through a verse which you have never noticed before but which speaks directly to your situation, perhaps with a command for you to obey. At other times you may notice a promise embedded in the passage, like a primrose hiding in the hedgerow in spring. Make it yours. Act on it. If a passage is an exuberant outburst of praise, try to enter into it with your intellect, your imagination, your senses. If life is dark, if your spiritual pilgrimage feels more like the aridity of the desert than the green pastures the Psalmist describes, then carry on reading, looking for a glimmer of encouragement or a flicker of hope. If the passage contains clear instructions concerning Christian behaviour, store it up in the retrieval system of your mind, or better still, record it in writing somewhere so that if ever you need to know the mind of God on this subject, the information is at your finger-tips.

*For example*

To show what I mean, let me illustrate from my own Bible reading in recent days. As I write this, I have just returned from holiday, refreshed, renewed. My love for God's Word has been rekindled. I am enjoying steeping myself in it.

The day after I arrived back from holiday, a friend telephoned to tell me that her husband, a clergyman, was having an affair with another woman. In my prayer for that situation, I asked God to show me how I could help. Perhaps I should write?

Two days later, a verse of Scripture from my planned reading pierced me like a sharp sword. 'So hear the word I speak and give them warning from me. When I say to the wicked, "O wicked man, you will surely die," and you do not speak out to dissuade him from his ways, that wicked man will die for his sin, and I will hold you accountable for his blood' (Ezekiel 33:7–8).

I shared this experience with a group of friends who were also praying for this couple so that they could test whether this was a word from God for this situation. Then I wrote the letter.

The following day, I was feeling keenly the imminent departure of our son, who was about to leave home, and our daughter who was in the throes of packing to return to College. Our big house seems desolate when they are not there. Nestling in the first verse of the Psalm that day I found this, 'In God alone there is rest for my soul, from him comes my safety; with him alone for my rock, my safety, my fortress, I can never fall' (Psalm 62:1, JB). It was the word 'rock' which spoke volumes to me. On holiday in Austria, I had been reflecting how the mountain towering over the farmstead where we were staying provided refuge for many of God's creatures: deer, rabbits, birds. It was an easy move, therefore, to step from desolation into the protective rock: Jesus.

The next day I was puzzling over this chapter asking, 'What do you want me to include, Lord? What shall I leave out?' My readings that morning included the verse from Colossians I have already quoted, 'Make sure that no-one traps you and deprives you of your freedom' (2:8, JB).

Alongside these verses and words which seemed to have been winged from heaven for me for those particular days, I was recording in my notebook specific commands and instructions which I and every Christian need to absorb until they become a part of the fibre of our life, like breath – 'Let us sing for joy to the LORD . . . Let us come before him with thanksgiving' (Psalm 95:1–2). 'Let us bow down in worship, let us kneel before the LORD our Maker' (95:6).

At the moment, with this encouragement in the forefront of my mind, I come to the Bible expecting God's Word to enrich me. Alas! It is not always like that. There are days – and weeks and months sometimes – when exploration of the Bible seems more like hard grind than this joyful bending to the wind of God's Word. Even so, if we store God's Word in our hearts and obey it, we are being enriched, changed, rescued by it, even though our feelings may discount this claim.

*A warning*
At this point, I must add a word of warning. There are perils attached to Bible reading. The chief peril is spiritual pride; or as C. S. Lewis puts it, 'priggery'. The spiritual prig pleads, 'Give us more teaching.' But the abundance of Bible knowledge, instead of providing a firm rule for life, inflates him with pride, the know-all pride the Lord so loathed in the Pharisees. The spiritual prig boasts about the number of Bible verses he has learnt by heart but pays no attention to the number of Bible commands he is seeking to obey. I am not knocking a genuine thirst for Bible teaching, nor pouring scorn on committing Scripture to memory. What I am saying is, Examine your motives. Let these disciplines be for one purpose only – that you may humbly obey the whole will of God.

The spiritual prig also claims, 'The Lord has told me . . .' and refuses to submit that so-called word from the Lord to others for testing. Beware of this temptation to spiritual pride. The Enemy is crouching at the door claiming many Christian lives in this way. Be excited by God's Word. Expect him to speak to you through it. But beware of becoming pride-puffed. And never use the Bible like a daily horoscope. Heed the Bible's clear injunction: test the spirits to see if they come from God (1 John 4:1). This includes testing whether what you *think* God is saying to you through his Word is an accurate interpretation. It is all too easy to twist Bible verses to force them to say what you want to hear.

*Examine it*
As we steep ourselves in God's Word, we shall want to examine it, to understand it as fully as possible. I cannot emphasize this enough in these days when many Christians, faced with the choice of a banquet or bread-crumbs, choose breadcrumbs when it comes to feeding on God's Word. God has spread before us a feast of teaching: it takes a lifetime to sample and savour all that the Bible contains. Don't let that daunt you; let it enthuse you. Beware of the crumby Christian mentality which is content with a verse here and a snippit of Scripture there. Determine to work your way through the entire Bible eventually, to enjoy it, learn from it, obey it.

If we are to come to the Bible expecting it to speak to us, we must be prepared for some hard work. We must ask certain questions, 'What does this passage or book really mean? Why did the writer express it in that way? Why did he choose that particular word? What was he intending to convey? What would it have communicated to the original readers? What does it imply for today's Christian? What is God saying to me?'.

In coming to terms with some of these penetrating questions, we shall want, from time to time, to reach for the commentaries, the concordances, the Bible dictionaries, to aid us in our understanding. This kind of Bible exploration is not only illuminating and challenging, it is thrilling. It is also time-consuming. Try to ear-mark at least an hour a week for this kind of essential spade-work. Set yourself goals. For example, if you are to live biblically, you must know what the Bible teaches about key areas of your life: marriage (if you are married or hope to be), sexuality, money, ambition, giving, service, handling temptation, to mention a few. Look up in a concordance the references to 'giving', for example. Discover the principles God is highlighting here, the thread which runs through the whole of the Bible's teaching. Resolve to bring your life into alignment with this teaching.

Or take a recurring theme, like 'Peace'. Discover where that word is used, what it means, so that Jesus' words, 'In me you may have peace' (John 16:33) cease to be a vague promise you cling to when the going is tough but instead become consoling and strengthening words which you understand and apply.

*Bible meditation*
Treated in this way, the Bible's resources are found to be endless. They feed us at every age and stage of our pilgrimage.

I have suggested that this in-depth Bible study should take place in addition to the normal Quiet Time, mainly

51

because it is time-consuming and can easily squeeze out the prayer which should also find its place in the daily devotional time. This does not mean that I am suggesting that for the rest of the week the commentaries, concordances and dictionaries should gather dust on your shelves. Of course not. Whether we are sitting and reading the Bible for the sheer pleasure of immersing ourselves in God's Word, or whether we are ruminating over a small portion of Scripture, our minds must be fully engaged and very often a Bible dictionary or good notes will enrich our meditation by deepening our understanding. But don't be in bondage to commentaries, notes, notebooks and the paraphernalia which so easily clutters our desk whenever we attempt to listen to God's Word. Allow the Bible to speak for itself. Always be prepared to move on in your question from, 'What can I learn *about* God?' to, 'How can I draw nearer to him? How can I love him more deeply? How can I demonstrate that love in day-to-day obedience?'

It may happen, as you read a particular passage from the Bible, that these questions are answered in an obvious, straightforward way. Take the Bible at face value. Its pithy commands are powerful: Do not commit adultery. Do not steal. Commands like these are to be acted upon unquestioningly.

There are other passages of the Bible, though, which yield the mystery of their message only to those who are prepared to spend time poring over the hidden meanings. Was this why the Psalmist meditated on the Bible day and night? In recent years I have also been discovering the value of Bible meditation: poring over a fragment of Scripture, applying my imagination and senses to it. It speaks, then, with such power that I want to suggest this method to you. You might try it alongside the other methods I have already mentioned.

Take Colossians 2:6–7, the passage I was reading this week, which I have already quoted:

> You must live your whole life according to the Christ you have received – Jesus the Lord; you must be rooted in him and built on him and held firm by the faith you have been taught, and full of thanks-giving . . . (JB).

The passage as it stood gripped and challenged me. But one little phrase intrigued me, 'be rooted in him'. I wanted to chew that phrase over, to ask God to speak to me through the richness of the language.

I therefore returned to that phrase and read it over and over, in its context, but as slowly as possible. Then I tried to respond to each word in turn.

'Be.' Here is a command, not an optional extra. I must sit up and take notice.

'Rooted.' My mind went back to Singapore where I had seen trees which to my mind were extraordinary. They pushed their roots out from the belly of the trunk, five feet above ground. These roots stretched their long arms down, down, to touch the soil and then burrow into it, thus forming a firm anchor for the growing tree. I thought, too, of the beech roots I had been walking over in the wooded hills of Austria; how the gnarled toes wound their way round boulders and shrubs in order to plunge themselves into the rich soil. I sensed the hard work involved and began to ask God to give me similar tenacity and determination. I tried to sense how it might feel if one could become a root pushing one's way below ground, searching for food to send up to the maturing fruit. A prayer was born. 'Lord, I want every part of me to co-operate with you that my life might be similarly anchored, fed and sustained.'

'In him.' The realization that the soil of my life, as it were, is Jesus, filled me with awe and wonder. Is there a safer plantation? Was ever soil so fertile? It spoke to me of the strength and resourcefulness of God which in turn filled me with fresh courage, renewed vigour and strength. I prayed that I might take these qualities into my world: to my family, my colleagues and the people who come to me for counselling.

Fanciful? Subjective? For me, it is a form of meditation God seems to use. I suspect it is not so very different from the method the Psalmist used. I therefore recommend it as a supplement to the regular Bible study I have already mentioned.

There are other forms of Bible meditation, but it would take more space to explain them than this chapter affords. I hope I have said enough here to encourage you to be flexible in your approach to God's Word, to enjoy it and to let it speak, not only to your mind, but to your senses and to your feelings also.

## The Jesus-centred life

Just as there is a whole world of difference between knowing the Bible and living biblically, so there is a huge difference between knowing about God and knowing him through Jesus. But if what the Bible says is true, the truth is not only the written Word, it is also a person. Jesus said, 'I am the way and the truth and the life' (John 14:6). 'The Holy Spirit, the source of all truth' (John

15:26, LB). If what the Bible says about the inter-relation between freedom and truth is also true, 'the truth will set you free' (John 8:32), then it follows that if we want to enjoy Christ's freedom, we must deepen our relationship with this person who *is* truth. Our obedience is not simply to the written Word, our obedience stems from full submission to the living Word, Jesus himself.

Is it possible to develop a relationship with someone whose essential nature is truth? Indeed it is. One of the emancipating things about God's Word is that it assures us that God desires to forge a friendship with us no matter how sinful, struggling or worthless we may feel ourselves to be. When friends spend time together, they grow to be alike. It is as we spend time with the truth that we learn to shed the imaginations and desires and deeds of sin's underworld. Instead we delight in the truth and all that he stands for. This is why friendship with Jesus is a life-changing encounter, a transforming friendship.

We need never think of the truth as a formidable foe, the prefect who watches and waits for us to put a foot wrong. On the contrary, Jesus, who is the truth, is also love. 'God is love.' Love transcends worthlessness and communicates acceptance, affirmation and commitment.

This dimension of love was brought home to me recently while watching television. The cameras zoomed in on a mother sitting by the bedside of one of her children, the twelfth. The child sat in the hospital bed whimpering like a frightened animal: helpless. From the waist up, the infant's emaciated body was covered with weeping sores and scorch marks. Her thin face was àlso discoloured and scarred: the effects of a bomb blast. Yet the mother leant over this scrap of suffering humanity and contemplated her with love. It was as though this child was the only one who had ever been born. It was as though this child was still the pretty little girl she had once been.

The Bible asserts that God's love for us is like that: constant, tender, transforming, committed. It encourages us to believe that we are the focus of God's active love. Ezekiel describes it poetically in chapter 16:6–14. Paul says something similar in Romans 8: 'Since we are God's children, we will possess the blessings he keeps for his people' (v.17 GNB). Jesus underlined the fact of his love time and time again, especially in the hours leading up to his death. He proclaimed the message in simple terms: 'I have loved you' (John 13:34; 15:12); 'I loved you' (John 15:9); 'I am coming back to you' (John 14:28).

We must never lose sight of the fact that Christian commitment is two-way. I commit myself to Jesus because he has already committed himself to me. He commits himself to me. His commitment is total.

There is no need, then, to fear closeness with the truth. But if we would know ourselves the object of his care, if we would know ourselves loved, forgiven, accepted by him, we must spend time with him. Prayer becomes a priority.


### Notes for chapter three

[1] Robert Van de Weyer, *Guru Jesus* (SPCK, 1975), p. 119.
[2] Robert Van de Weyer, p. 129.
[3] C. S. Lewis, *Reflections on the Psalms* (Fontana, 1961), p. 53.

# 4

# *Freedom in prayer*

Prayer is a many-faceted activity. There is space here to focus on only one facet, a neglected one. I refer to the prayer which is the unashamed attempt at deepening our knowledge of Jesus; opening ourselves to him.

This prayer is not complicated. It is a gift. A gift is a present given by one person to another. A gift is something to be received. Often, we have to learn how to use a gift. This gift, prayer, is a present from God, to be received and explored. We will look, all too briefly, at the 'how to' of exploring a relationship with the God who desires this friendship so much more than we ever do; the God who comes.

## Developing a friendship with God

Of course, all friends discover their own methods of growing more intimate with one another. The same is true of closeness with God. But over the years, while I have been exploring this life-giving dimension of prayer, I have found myself returning again and again to seven stages of prayer. I share them here so that if you are serious about exposing your life to the truth you may experiment with them for yourself.[1]

## 1 *Relaxation*

A relationship between friends grows when they relax together. We need to learn to relax with Jesus; not to rush in and out of his presence with a nod and a mere 'Good Morning, God', but rather to be still before him. As the Psalmist put it, 'Be still, and know that I am God' (Psalm 46:10). Sit down. Or kneel. Allow your body to express openness to God. Unclench your hands. Unwind in the presence of God. Remind yourself that he is the truth. Remind yourself that he wants you to pray more than you do. Remind yourself that he is already praying for you. Remember that perfect love is what God is. Use some verses of Scripture to bring you into this awareness, for example: 'I know that my Redeemer lives' (Job 19:25); 'God is our refuge and strength, an ever present help in trouble' (Psalm 46:1); 'Great is the LORD, and most worthy of praise' (Psalm 48:1); 'Let us come before him with thanksgiving' (Psalm 95:2).

## 2 *Reflection*

Reflect on the amazing fact that Jesus is present with you. Your name is graven on the palms of his hands. You are never out of his mind. His eye of love is always on you. He cares for you. He is the vine, you are a branch. You dwell in him and he dwells in you. His life is in you like sap rising to feed and renew the branch. His Spirit is praying for you now (see Romans 8:26–27). He loves you better than you love yourself. He knows you

58

better than you know yourself. He accepts you as you are. He is using this prayer to change you into his own likeness. Again, pre-selected verses of Scripture can aid this phase of prayer. 'I am the vine; you are the branches' (John 15:5); 'You did not choose me, but I chose you' (John 15:16); 'The word of God (Jesus) lives in you' (1 John 2:14); 'The eternal God is your refuge, and underneath are the everlasting arms' (Deuteronomy 33:27).

## 3 *Response*
Surrender every part of yourself to him. Consciously yield the whole of yourself to him: the response of love to Love. Hand over your talents, your attitudes, your values, your thoughts, your imagination, your decisions, your friendships and every part of your body to him. Determine to allow no part of you to return to sin's bondage. Rather, make a conscious choice: all that is mine will become his. 'Take me and all I have. Do with me whatever you will. Send me where you will. Use me as you will. I surrender myself and all I possess absolutely and entirely, unconditionally and forever to your control.'

Allow your own thoughts and plans to fade into the background. Instead, see his plan. Then endeavour to cut your life according to his pattern; not out of duty, but out of love. 'Lord, this is what *I* wanted. But now, not my will, rather yours be done.' This may produce a struggle, but when the struggle is over the joy and peace of obedience will be as refreshing as a long, cool drink in summer.

## 4 *Recognition*
Recognize that Jesus was there, calling you into his felt presence before you ever decided to come to this place of prayer. The initiative was not yours, it was his. 'Then the

man and his wife heard the sound of the LORD God as he was walking in the garden in the cool of the day, and they hid from the LORD God among the trees of the garden. But the LORD God called to the man, "Where are you?"' (Genesis 3:8–9). 'We love because he first loved us' (1 John 4:19). 'But while he was still a long way off, his father saw him and was filled with compassion for him; he ran to his son, threw his arms around him and kissed him' (Luke 15:20). Thank him that he calls, watches, waits, and yearns for you to come. Be aware of anything which keeps you apart. Be ready to allow him to remove that barrier: an attitude, a grudge, an obsession, a friendship. Allow him to do what he will. Allow him to express his love for you in any way he chooses. Wait for him to speak to you.

## 5 Recollection

Recall that Jesus is praying for you now. I find it helps me to have that fact written up in my study where I spend much of my day in counselling and writing. 'Jesus is praying for me now.' My prayer depends, not so much on my technique as on him and his ceaseless activity before the throne of grace. 'Christ Jesus . . . is at the right hand of God and is also interceding for us' (Romans 8:34). 'He always lives to intercede for them' (Hebrews 7:25).

Remember that Paul speaks of prayer as a gift. You don't have to strive in this relationship. Hand over the reins to the Holy Spirit who is praying for you (Romans 8:26–27). Trust God to interpret accurately all the sighs, groans, wordlessness, even tears which may express what you want to say more adequately than words. Be open to the re-creative love of God which is at work within you, as unobtrusive yet as effective as yeast leavening dough, or salt and herbs drawing out the flavour of a casserole.

## 6 *Repentance*

We must come to God as we are. We cannot pretend to him. We must be real. We are sinful; spiritual cripples, disabled, impoverished and soiled in so many ways: in our bodies, minds and spirits. We lay our sin at the foot of his cross. Then we hold up our hands in penitence and faith. We recall the good news: God looks, not on our sin, but on the sacrifice of his Son. He sees us as though we were persons who had never sinned. We will not nurse a sense of guilt, therefore. We will abandon guilt, sin and discouragement into his immense, unending love. We will turn away from our sin, walk away from it – to Jesus. We will go free. We will receive his forgiveness, acceptance and embrace.

## 7 *Receptivity*

God responds. He turns to me. He seeks me. He speaks to me. He fills me afresh with his Spirit. I receive all that he has for me: joy, guidance, encouragement, peace. I bask in the assurance of his love. I submit all that I know of myself to all that I know of him: the Truth. His presence brings a deep, spiritual calm, a greater serenity, an ability to accept and even to suffer, an ability to detach myself from all that is unhelpful, to hear his rebuke. His presence provides a new perspective. He, the source of truth, draws me deeper into truth, into the truth which sets people free.

Does this sound me-centred, utterly subjective, a self-indulgent waste of time? It can be. It can become sheer escapism. On the other hand, this kind of prayer, when accompanied by a working knowledge of the Bible, can become a resourceful encounter with the living God, just as prayer was for Jesus.

Through prayer, God furnishes us with the nerve we need to re-enter the hurly-burly of the world. Through prayer, he provides the strength we need to win in our struggle against the head wind of temptation, disappointment and persistent failure. Through prayer, the Holy Spirit renews our perspective, enabling us to view much that puzzles and perplexes from a Godward angle. Prayer gives access to the source of pure love: the love we then carry back with us into the loveless world.

Prayer, then, becomes the undercurrent of our life. It sweeps us along in a Godward direction. But this kind of prayer requires time and application. To drop into the stillness I have described, you must allow yourself an uncluttered, undisturbed ten minutes; preferably longer. But once you have learnt the art of being still before God, recognizing his presence, you will find you can steal into this empowering silence anywhere and at any time of day: walking to lectures; feeding the baby: riding on the bus; washing-up. You discover that this ability to cultivate your friendship with the God who dwells within you at the core of your personality requires, not so much an absence of noise, as an attitude of heart.

The prayer which is friendship with God also demands courage – the courage to do as Jesus suggested, to go into your room alone, shut the door and work at a friendship with one whom you love but have never seen. That is one reason why, as well as praying alone, we need to pray with other Christians from time to time. We shall go on to look at this need in greater detail.

## Refreshment through obedience

Prayer not only requires time and courage, but demands our obedience. As we have seen, prayer is a love relationship between the believer and God. The test of this love is obedience. Jesus said, 'If you love me, you will obey what I command' (John 14:15). Those who are in rebellion against God, those who set out to thwart his authority, those who are determined to fight God, to test their strength against his, and those who defy his laws, will make no progress in this kind of prayer. Only those who are serious in their desire to be transformed by the truth will appreciate its beauty, endure its refining pain and submit to the hand of love which is also the hand which disciplines (see Hebrews 12:6). The paradox is that only those who are captivated by the truth enjoy God's freedom.

In this chapter we have observed that the truth is a person: Jesus. The truth is God's Word, the Bible. The truth is God's Word pressed home to our personal situation by the Holy Spirit. The Christian who would know truth's liberating energy must not only know the truth but resolve to be held captive by it. 'I will be careful to lead a blameless life' (Psalm 101:2). Then, and only then, can God's truth set us free.

A letter, a quick visit or a phone-call from someone you love can raise your spirits instantly, keep you going for days. Through prayer, Bible study and the indwelling Holy Spirit we have a similar spiritual life-line: instant access to God. 'We have, then, my brothers, complete freedom to go into the Most Holy Place by means of the death of Jesus . . . So let us come near to God with a sincere heart and a sure faith' (Hebrews 10:19, 22, GNB).

While this book has been taking shape, two vital truths have clicked into place for me. They have always been there in the fuzziness of the background of my mind. Now they are in the foreground in sharp perspective. The first is this. For Christian pilgrims intent on journeying into freedom, Holy-Spirit-inspired prayer and Bible reading are the vital, renewable refreshment we must take if we are to survive the trip. Like the constant flow of an underground stream or the gentle fall of heavy dew in summer, their work in us is unseen; hidden but essential. And the second? One of Satan's most subtle ploys is to persuade Christians to view prayer and Bible reading as a chore, a duty. The word 'duty' carries kill-joy overtones for most of us. Chores are things to be dispensed with as quickly and mindlessly as possible, like washing-up or cleaning the car. We even find ourselves resenting dutiful chores and viewing them as interruptions to real life, begrudging the time they take. As we observed in the previous chapter, it is one of the tragedies of today's climate that Christians have ceased to think of prayer and Bible reading as delights, valuable assets, the privileged open sesame to God. Instead they delegate these disciplines to the super-keen, pursue prayerless lives and wonder why they are not achieving their full potential in Christ. We shall never experience Christian growth until we commit ourselves to the twin delights of prayer and Bible reading. The purpose of this chapter is to encourage you to discover for yourself how you can fit personal prayer, Bible reading, spiritual reading and shared prayer into an already full diary. It is possible; possible and desirable. As Bishop Theophan, a teacher of prayer in the nineteenth century, used to say, 'When Prayer is right, everything is right.'

## How do I find time to pray?

Some Christians reading chapter three of this book may have been tempted to despair. How *does* busy modern man make time for all this conscious God-awareness? Some of you who read this book will be genuinely stretched for time and drained of emotional resources. I think of those friends of mine to whom this applies: Iain, a long-distance lorry driver who starts work at six-thirty, or earlier, every morning and arrives home in the evening zombie-like; Pam, an occupational therapist in a large mental hospital who rises at six and comes in at night drained by the demands of her job; Diana, a young mother with an adorable but demanding five-month-old baby who loves to play rather than sleep. How *do* such people find time to benefit from the spiritual resource points of prayer, Bible meditation and the Spirit's daily in-filling? There are three major requirements: an attitude, a strategy and a rhythm.

*An attitude*
We always find time to do what we want to do. In fact you can learn a great deal about a person by examining his priorities. Two people who love each other somehow create time to be alone together. Two young friends of mine even have breakfast together most days, so strong is their yearning to get to know one another well.

Do you believe in the sustaining ingredient of prayer? Do you want to expose yourself to this life-enriching, life-transforming activity of God's Spirit? Do you really want to obey the Bible's many commands to pray: 'Be still, and know that I am God' (Psalm 46:10); 'When you pray, go into your room, close the door' (Matthew 6:6); 'This is my Son, whom I love. Listen to him!' (Mark 9:7); 'When you pray, say: "Father"' (Luke 11:2); 'They should always pray and not give up' (Luke 18:1).

If your response to these questions is positive, it surely follows that prayer must become a regular part of your diet, as normal and regular as the daily intake of food? If you believe in prayer, you will carve out a space for it. But don't be lulled into thinking that because prayer is to become routine it has to become boring. On the contrary, just as a routine job can provide you with the stimulation which both stretches and fulfils you, so prayer can be just as exciting if you come to it with a spirit of eager anticipation. God surely encourages us to adopt this attitude when he makes his profound promise through Isaiah, 'As the rain and the snow come down from heaven, and do not return to it without watering the earth and making it bud and flourish, so that it yields seed for the sower and bread for the eater, so is my word that goes out from my mouth: It will not return to me empty, but will accomplish what I desire and achieve the purpose for which I sent it' (Isaiah 55:10–11). What is true of God's written Word, the Bible, is also true of the living Word, God's Son. When you really encounter him in prayer, you cannot remain the same.

If this is God's truth, if prayer and Bible reading are essential to our spiritual growth, then it is vital that we ask God to renew our perception of prayer and our perception of him. God is not a demanding, cantankerous Patriarch sitting in the heavenly places clutching a stop-watch, clocking up the hours we spend on our knees or perusing the Scriptures. On the contrary, God is the generous giver who waits to replenish our dwindling resources from his plentiful supply. Everything we need for the journey into freedom, the journey we embarked on at conversion, is to be found in him. Those who receive from him are those who ask, those who come. Those who come daily into his presence receive rich rewards. If you are serious in your intent to become one of God's freedom fighters, to borrow David Watson's phrase, it is folly to attempt to survive without these fresh God-touches. But if you are to open yourself to God's intervention in your life on a regular basis, you must make strategic plans. Life sweeps us along. Circumstances dictate the pace unless we take a firm grip and plan ahead.

*A strategy*
If you are serious about making time for God, three things are necessary. You must plan your day, plan your week, and know yourself.

As we saw in chapter three, what is required is that we discover a time to be still before God, to absorb his Word, to listen to him speaking through Christian literature, to pray with others. The first thing to discover is whether you are the reflective kind of person who prefers a prolonged period of quietness, or whether you are the extrovert with a butterfly brain who concentrates for a maximum of ten minutes and then flits to another flower. Be self-aware. Be realistic. Let your prayer pattern match your personality. Other methods might work well for other people but they are not for you. You are in pursuit of a prayer-pattern which is workable in your unique situation.

Just as self-awareness is an asset when this prayer-planning process is undergoing an overhaul, so honesty is vital. Are you awake, alert, before eleven in the morning? If not, don't make that your major prayer time. Instead, discover the time of day when you are alert, yet relaxed. Ear-mark that: 'God-time'. Fifteen minutes with God at that time will be more productive than two hours in the early morning if your ability to concentrate then is nil. God doesn't mind *when* you come. Jesus is interceding for you the entire day anyway. But it does matter to him that at some stage in the day you deliberately lay worldly concerns on one side and come face to face with him, focusing on him. It matters to him about you. So when will you do this?

Pam, the occupational therapist I mentioned earlier, showed me her timetable recently. Writing it out like this is a helpful way to see at a glance where time for prayer can be made.

*Pam's day:*

| | |
|---|---|
| 6.05 | Alarm rings. |
| 6.10 ish | Get out of bed. Quick wash. |
| 6.20 | Quiet Time: prayer, Bible meditation, spiritual reading. |
| 6.50 | Get dressed. Make bed. |
| 7.00 | Breakfast. |
| 7.15–20 | Leave house. |
| 7.30 | Catch bus. Ten minutes alone with God, continuing my Quiet Time before colleagues get on the same bus. |

| | |
|---|---|
| 8.30 | Check-in at work. Change into uniform. |
| 8.45 | Work starts. |
| 10.00 | Tea break. |
| 10.20 | Work with mentally handicapped patients. |
| 12.00 | Lunch. |
| 12.45 | End of lunch-break. Work with patients. |
| 3.00 | Tea break. |
| 3.20 | Work with patients. |
| 4.30 | Leave work. |
| 5.15 | Arrive home shattered. Make sandwiches for tomorrow's lunch. If I'm not cooking for the others in the house I go to my room and pray over the events of the day. I feel a great need to be alone at this time. |
| 6.00 | Tea-time with the other four girls in the house. Chat with them. Wash up. |
| 7.30–8.00 | Free time to do odd jobs: laundry, ironing, housework, letter-writing. |
| 9.30–9.45 | Get ready for bed. |
| 10.15–10.30 | Collapse into bed. Lights out. |

This is a typical day for Pam; but of course her programme changes from day to day. On Tuesdays, for example, her colleagues go shopping in the lunch break. She stays in the staff room where she is able to use the time for Bible study or meditation. On Tuesday evenings she prays with the other girls in the house for mutual support and on Thursday evenings she attends a Bible study group organized by her church.

The physical tiredness which dogs Pam as a result of being on her feet all day, coupled with the mental and emotional tiredness which arises because of the nature of her work, gave rise to an inner struggle. At one stage she was asking in some despair, 'How *can* I make prayer a priority?' As you can see, she has made it a priority mainly because she has a hunger for God which mere circumstances, demanding as they are, cannot quench. She has created a sacred space in each day when she can commune with God, listen to him and be changed by him. She is also refusing to allow the pressure of time to squeeze out prayer with others.

Pam's weekends are also busy: shopping, chores, seeing friends, helping at church. But this is the only time she has for Bible study. Her next task is to plot a fixed point, maybe fortnightly or monthly, when she can reach for the commentaries and enjoy the luxury of leisurely Bible study. In Pam's case, it may be necessary for her to prune her Sunday activities to give herself time for this irreplaceable spiritual food.

*John's day:*
Another friend of mine, John, wrote down his timetable for me. His day is very different:

| | |
|---|---|
| 7.45–8.00 | Get up. |
| 8.00–8.15 | Wash. Shave. Dress. Make bed. |
| 8.15–8.45 | Breakfast. |
| 8.45 | Leave for work – a leisurely walk. |
| 9.00 | Arrive at work. Busy until lunch-time. |
| 1.00 | Lunch. |
| 2.00 | Work. |
| 3.45 | Tea-break on some days. |
| 4.00 | Work. |
| 5.30 | Leave work. Walk home. |
| 5.45 | Arrive home. |

| 5.45–7.15 | Prepare and eat dinner. Evening free for a variety of activities. |
| 11.00–11.15 | Prepare for bed: horlicks and cheese. |
| 11.30–12.00 | Quiet Time in bed. |
| 12.00 | Lights out. |

John's day, if planned imaginatively, provides plenty of scope for prayer. By cutting four minutes from breakfast-time, he could drop into some silence with God before he leaves the house. He usually walks to and from work alone, which gives him two fifteen-minute prayer walks during which a great deal of intercession can take place. At lunch-time, a quiet room is available where he can go. This is an excellent place for Bible meditation, spiritual reading or quiet prayer. Then, Saturdays and Sundays are his own. With careful planning, an hour of Bible study could be slotted in each week. And, of course, many of his routine activities: shaving, bed-making, dressing, require little conscious thought. They, too, could become occasions when he tunes in to God.

On Thursday mornings, John meets with two friends before breakfast for prayer, sharing and support. On Tuesday evenings he attends a church fellowship and Bible study group.

Time is available. The crunch question is, 'Do I want to seize every available opportunity to turn my eyes God-wards as Jesus seemed to do?'

My own experience of prayer persuades me of the value of what we used to call breadcrumbs: the odd five minutes used rather than wasted, redeemed by prayer or Scripture-ruminating rather than frittered away in idleness because 'you can't do anything useful in five minutes'. The fact is that five minutes is quite long enough to equip yourself with spiritual armour, to reach God-wards for a fresh in-filling of his Holy Spirit, to read a paragraph from a helpful book such as Ulrich Schaffer's *Into Your Light*, Jim Packer's *Knowing God*, Richard Foster's *Celebration of Discipline*. These are life-changing books. Those wasted five minutes could become, then, a series of life-changing minutes.

*A rhythm*

When we plan our day, our week, our month in this way, plotting prayer points as well as work schedules and relaxation, we begin to live rhythmically. A person who moves rhythmically moves with ease, purpose and quiet efficiency. There is a calm and an attractive poise about such a person. He knows where he is going and he gets there. He is free. This stands in stark contrast to the person who muddles through life because he is swept along by one demand after another. Such a person is far from free. He becomes enslaved to the demands of others, the demands of life, the clamour of self. Like a ship which has lost its anchor, this person is not free but hopelessly adrift. Jesus, though pressurized, was free to live rhythmically: to move in and out of the harbour of his Father's felt presence with ease and confidence. This is the freedom of access he wants us to enjoy also.

Is this why he commanded us to find a place (Matthew 6:6), to use a framework (Luke 11:2), to keep in tune? These could become spiritual anchor points, giving us security in the storms of life.

Purposeful people find a place in which to pray.

The Christians I met in Singapore were superb examples of this. Many live in overcrowded high-rise apartments. Most share a bedroom with at least one other member of the family, often a Buddhist. Yet such is their zeal for the Lord and for prayer that these Christians find a place: a spot under a tree in one of Singapore's public parks; the office, before work begins; a patch of grass on the way to the bus stop. We, too, must use our imagination and find a place. The place may be a corner of the bedroom, a chair in the study, a quiet room in the house. We know when we retreat to that place that this is for one purpose only: the serious business of prayer. That is not to say that we cannot pray anywhere and everywhere. Of course we can. God is not limited by our prayer-place. But it does mean that our rhythm of prayer is aided by establishing a particular prayer spot to which we retreat regularly. Christians who are married or who share a house with others need this quite as much as others. As one young wife put it to me recently, 'When I'm sitting in that chair my husband knows why I'm there. He protects my privacy with God and doesn't disturb me.'

*A flexible framework*
Similarly, people who adopt a flexible framework of prayer go places with God. Prayer should not degenerate into a sloppy, slip-shod, unthought-out burbling of random thoughts. Rather, prayer is imploring God to work in the very core of your being.

Jesus provided us with a valuable framework when he gave us the Lord's Prayer. Prayer is recollection: 'This is how you should pray: "Our Father".' Prayer is relinquishment: 'Your will be done.' Prayer is requesting: 'Give us today our daily bread.' Prayer includes repentance: 'Forgive us our debts.' Prayer includes a renunciation of evil: 'Deliver us from the evil one.' Prayer includes rejoicing: 'For yours is the kingdom and the power and the glory . . .' (Matthew 6:9ff.). Use this framework. Experiment with it. Make it yours by changing it. Or find a framework which suits you better. Sharpen up your prayer life so that it provides opportunities for God to work as deeply in you as you ask him to work in others. Prayer is not so much about changing the world as changing me so that I can be God's agent in the world. Prayer not only provides me with free access to God, but through it I give God free access to myself.

### Note for chapter four

[1] Although I would not endorse all its teaching, I am indebted to a booklet, now out of print, by James Borst, entitled *A Method of Contemplative Prayer* (The Asian Trading Corporation, 1973) for the kernel of this method of quiet prayer.

# 5

# *The Holy Spirit and freedom*

Jesus is Lord! That triumphant boast is scrawled across banners and T-shirts these days. On one occasion I even saw the words adorning an Anglican bishop's vestments.

It is a simple matter to jump on the bandwagon and join the crowds who rejoice in this claim. To allow Jesus truly to reign in our lives, to give him the submission from which Christian freedom is born, is quite a different matter.

In chapters three and four we observed the importance to the believer of prayer and Bible knowledge. Without these there is no direct contact with the truth which stands worldly philosophy on its head and strips us of pretence: there is no conscious contact with the God who, so we claim, occupies the throne of our lives. Prayer? The Bible? But surely the Bible encourages us to believe that the Holy Spirit is the liberator? 'Where the Spirit of the Lord is, there is freedom' (2 Corinthians 3:17). Surely, then, if we are to discover our full potential as Christians, we must open ourselves fully to the Holy Spirit?

This question was puzzling one girl when she came to see me. 'I'm really confused these days. I hear these voices in my head, you see, and I see these visions. I think it's the Holy Spirit speaking to me. I'm trying hard to learn to listen so that I know what the Spirit wants me to do. But now I don't know whether to be guided by the Spirit or to carry on reading the Bible.'

## The Spirit: faithful to the Word of God

The answer to that problem is quite straightforward. Jesus put it in a nutshell: 'Your word is truth' (John 17:17). Paul elaborated, 'All Scripture is God-breathed and is useful for teaching, rebuking, correcting and training in righteousness' (2 Timothy 3:16). The Holy Spirit, the source of truth, will not therefore say anything which runs contrary to God's written Word, the Bible. Any inner voice which *does* whisper words which cannot be substantiated by Scripture must be ruled out of court. It is not the voice of the Holy Spirit.

Jim Packer puts the situation well.

The Spirit of Christ who indwells Christians never leads them to doubt, criticize, go beyond or fall short of Bible teaching. Spirits which do that are not the Spirit of Christ (1 John 4:1–6). Rather, the Spirit makes us appreciate the divine authority of Scripture, so that we accept its account of spiritual realities and live as it calls us to do . . . Never does the Spirit draw us away from the written Word, any more than from the living Word. Instead, he keeps us in constant, conscious, contented submission to both together. He exerts his authority precisely by making real to us the authority of Christ and of Scripture – more precisely, the authority of Christ *through* Scripture.[1]

If you want to test whether the voices inside you are Holy Spirit promptings, ask yourself some searching questions. Be honest. 'Am I allowing Jesus to reign in the nitty-gritty details of my life? Do I love his Word? Do I love him, not just with sentimental, content-less, slushy emotion but with glad obedience?' The Holy Spirit's task is to free us to love God in thought, word and deed; to free us, too, to love the truth, God's written Word. The Spirit's work is *not* to set us free from obedience to the Bible, as we shall go on to see in a later chapter.

## No need for fear

This is why there is no need to fear either the freedom the Holy Spirit gives, or his power. Fear, I find, is the chief barrier Christians put up in a desperate attempt to compartmentalize the Spirit's work in their lives. They are afraid of anyone else holding life's reins – even the Spirit of God.

I understand this fear. I used to share it. Then I realized that what really alarmed me was not the Holy Spirit's authentic ministry but the eccentric manifestations of that so-called ministry displayed by extrovert people. When I realized that Jesus, the most free, Spirit-filled person who ever walked this earth, neither swung from the chandeliers in the Temple, nor chased up and down Jerusalem shouting 'Hallelujah', I relaxed. If the Holy Spirit's intention was to make me more like Jesus (2 Corinthians 3:18), then, of course, he must be given access to all of me.

I realized, too, that the word 'power' need hold no terror and no stigma. The Holy Spirit's power has many faces. Sometimes it is cataclysmic, like an electrifying thunder-storm. At other times it is as gentle as a kiss. God is surely wise enough to discern what manner of power will match and enhance my personality.

## To be filled with the Spirit means to be filled with God

Are you afraid of the Holy Spirit's potential in you? Are you afraid to open yourself to his emancipating influence? Relax. Consider who he is. The Spirit of God means the breath, personality, energy of Jesus himself. To be filled with the Holy Spirit means to be filled with the life of God; Christlike-ness.

Robert Frost highlights some of the Holy Spirit's characteristics. 'Only a *lovely* person can minister *love* . . . Only a *joyful* person can minister *joy* . . . Only a *peaceful* person can minister *peace* . . . Only a *hopeful* person can minister *hope*.'[2] If we are to drive full throttle into freedom, the Holy Spirit must be handed the controls.

William Temple painted the picture well:

It is no good giving me a play like Hamlet or King Lear, and telling me to write a play like that. Shakespeare could do it; I can't. And it is no good showing me a life like the life of Jesus and telling me to live a life like that. Jesus could do it; I can't. But if the genius of Shakespeare could come and

78

live in me, then I could write plays like that. And if the Spirit of Jesus could come and live in me, I could live a life like that.[3]

*If* the Spirit of Jesus could come? This enabling Spirit has come. This is the good news Paul proclaims. The reason we can be assured of God's love for us is this: 'God has poured out his love into our hearts by the Holy Spirit, whom he has given us' (Romans 5:5). 'The Spirit of God lives in you. And if anyone does not have the Spirit of Christ, he does not belong to Christ' (Romans 8:9).

The liberating Spirit, then, indwells us whether we recognize his transforming presence or not. But he needs to fill us continually and release us in order that we might live life, not dictated by the demands of the flesh, but in obedience to Jesus. This is his life-long task. Contrary to much popular teaching which represents him as the member of the Holy Trinity whose work is only to inspire joy, hallelujah-chanting and hand-clapping, his work in us is painstaking, often painful and always challenging. He does bring us joy. And peace. And hope. (Romans 15:13.) But this need not be expressed in frothy, soap-sudsy emotionalism. It can be exuberant. On the other hand it can be, and very often is, too deep for words; mysterious, like mountains reflected in the still waters of a lake.

What happens to the believer who takes seriously Paul's command, 'Be filled with the Spirit' (Ephesians 5:18)? How does the Holy Spirit, the liberator, go about bringing us into ever-greater freedom? What is his part in enabling us to become more Christ-like?

*He convinces us of sin*

One of the first lessons we learn if we are heading for Christian freedom is that the Holy Spirit does exactly what Jesus foretold. He convinces us of sin (see John 16:8). Unless we are aware that this convicting work is as essential to our freedom as sand-papering is to decorating, we may not merely wonder what is happening to us, but may resent the Holy Spirit's intervention in our lives. I discovered this to my cost some nine years ago.

It was one of those periods in my Christian pilgrimage when my soul cried out for an awareness of God like parched earth cries out for warm rain in summer. 'Lord, drench me with the water of your Holy Spirit if that's what I need.'

I don't know what I expected God to do. Pour strength and peace into the withered places, perhaps? Give me a warm sense of his love?

What I do know is that I grew indignant with God's apparent inactivity. No strength came. No peace flooded my soul. Rather, a horrifying awareness of my own sinfulness crept over me so that I saw myself as I really was: a sinner, coated with grime.

It wasn't that I had committed any of the spectacular sins like adultery or murder or theft. Ordinary, humdrum, grubby little sins had accumulated without my noticing. After all, I had been too busy *serving* God to be over-conscious of sin. But now I saw it and felt cheated. Where was the promised energizing the Holy Spirit was supposed to inject (Acts 1:8)? I remember praying, 'Lord, I asked you for more of your Spirit's life and power. All you have given me is an awareness of sin; not even anyone else's sin. My own!'

Eventually the truth dawned. God had answered my

original prayer – 'Drench me with your Spirit.' But the Spirit convicts us of sin. I had not bargained for this outcome and certainly failed to welcome it.

## He purges us from sin

Why had I failed to appreciate that Holy-Spirit-freedom might diminish as well as up-build? If I had stopped to consider, I would have known that the *Holy* Spirit would not co-exist with sin. If I had stopped to think, I would have remembered that his work is a purging work. 'When he (the Holy Spirit) comes, he will convict the world of guilt in regard to sin' (John 16:8). But the full significance of this word, 'convict', 'convince', 'reprove', had not filtered into my spiritual awareness.

Bible scholars tell us that this word, 'convict', was the word customarily used for the cross-examination of a witness or a man on trial. It always has the idea of cross-examining a person until that person admits his wrong-doing.[4]

What Jesus is promising in this verse is that when the Holy Spirit's energy operates in our lives, he will pin us against the wall, as it were, until we acknowledge our waywardness and recognize the seedlings of sin which spring up, albeit unbidden, in our hearts. Or, to put it another way, the Holy Spirit will come into the dark, hidden, secret crevices of our souls, switch on his spotlight and expose all the murky fantasies, desires, ambitions and hopes which have lurked there. To change the metaphor again, he will wound us, if necessary, to cut away the terrifying crust of sin which quickly coats even the child of God; which threatens to eradicate the hard-won freedom Christ died that we might enjoy. His

81

purpose? To keep us free from sin; to prevent us from falling prey once more to sin's captivity (Galatians 5:1), to make of our lives a greater capacity for God.

### He jolts us into obedience

This goading work of the Holy Spirit is part of his role as 'the Comforter'. As David Watson reminds us, 'the Comforter' does not simply denote the helper who comes alongside us in our afflictions, though it does mean that. 'The Comforter' is also one who afflicts us in our comfortableness, prods us in our complacency and jolts us out of a slip-shod life-style into a joyfully obedient one.

### He washes us clean

And the purifying work of the Spirit is included in the Bible's use of the term 'baptism'. 'He will baptize you with the Holy Spirit' (Mark 1:8). Baptism is a sign of initiation, but its fulfilment is also an ongoing process. As Robert Frost helpfully points out, the word 'baptism' includes a ceremonial washing. It is used by Mark to describe the washing of pots, cups and copper bowls (Mark 7:4). It is also used to describe Naaman's ceremonial cleansing and purifying when he bathed in the River Jordan (2 Kings 5:14).

The Spirit's convicting, purging, goading, purifying work spells freedom. When his activity leaves its inevitable mark on your soul, do not despise or belittle yourself. Read the signs for what they are: the forerunners of freedom, the Spirit's preparation. You are being prepared for ultimate freedom, you are being prepared to become the Bride of Christ.

## Free to bear fruit

The Holy Spirit is like a thorough gardener. He is orderly. He sweeps leaves from the paths of life and burns them. Where he is in control, soil is kept fertile through weeding. And the pruning-knife is not spared. He frees the garden for fruitfulness.

Soil is kept fertile through weeding. When we turned to Christ, sin was rampant. Like bindweed, it appeared everywhere and from nowhere: 'Sexual immorality, impurity and debauchery; idolatry and witchcraft; hatred, discord, jealousy, fits of rage, selfish ambition, dissensions, factions and envy; drunkenness, orgies, and the like' (Galatians 5:19–21). But, as Paul warns us, 'Those who live like this will not inherit the kingdom of God' (Galatians 5:21).

The Holy Spirit must therefore regularly control these enemies of our soul which threaten to choke, strangle and overpower the likeness of Jesus in us. But his work in us is not purely negative: to uproot. It is also gloriously productive: to produce fruit. The purging is for fruit-bearing. His spade does dig deep to remove stubborn tap-roots. But the Spirit's fingers also reach deep to implant God-seed in their place: love, joy, peace, patience, kindness, goodness, faithfulness, gentleness and self-control (Galatians 5:22). This fruit does not appear willy-nilly on the tree of our life. It must be cultivated with skill and with care. This is the Holy Spirit's work.

For the love Paul describes is Jesus' love, the unselfish affection and orientation which always promotes the well-being of others. The joy Paul describes is Jesus' joy, the ability to rejoice in spite of irksome circumstances, trying people or persistent pain. The peace Paul describes is Jesus' peace, the heart-knowledge which entrusts all things to the wisdom, sovereignty and omniscience of God. Patience (long-suffering), the ability to keep on enduring that which one does not enjoy, is Christ-likeness. Gentleness, the ability to place oneself in another's shoes and so identify with his feelings that no needless pain is inflicted; the ability to dispense with rudeness, harshness or abrasiveness, is Christ-likeness. Goodness, the freedom to reject all that is not of God, is Christ-likeness. Faithfulness is the loyalty, reliability, dependability and commitment which never disappoints and never lets another down; it is the quality which can assure another, 'When I say I'll be your friend, I'll always be your friend' and it was modelled to us by Jesus. Self-control – the ability to hear the clamour of one's own rebel emotions and inner needs coupled with the skill to know which to discipline and which to meet – was patterned to us only by Jesus in whom body, mind and soul were in perfect working order.

This is spiritual fruit, the fruit of freedom. Jesus' life was a spiritual harvest. But for us, harvest-time follows the fallowness of winter, the sap-rising of spring and the mellowing of summer. The process cannot be rushed. Freedom comes slowly, gradually, with maturity.

## Be filled with the Spirit

Even a cursory glance at Paul's fruit-stall is enough to convince the believer that, of himself, he is not capable of producing the goods. Then what is to happen? Paul tells us in Ephesians 5:18, 'be filled with the Spirit'. Let his sap rise within your life and together you can do it.

The Spirit's in-filling has a wide variety of meanings. Among others, it means to keep on being drenched, soaked, marinated, in the Spirit.

Our spiritual life may be likened to a sponge. When a sponge is left out of water for any length of time, it becomes hard, dry and ugly. When it is held in water, every cell, every fibre, softens and swells.

If we would live fruitfully, if we would become whole, free, we must allow our lives to be held regularly in the waters of the Holy Spirit so that his life penetrates ours, so that his life gradually transforms ours: our thought-patterns, affections, attitudes and ambitions. This regular in-filling is not mystical, me-centred or meaningless. No. It is essentially practical, as Jim Wallis warns. This movement of the Spirit is not theoretical or abstract: 'It has to do with very concrete things . . . He concerns himself with money, possessions, power, violence, anxiety, sexuality, faith and the law, security, true or false religion, the way we treat our neighbours, and the way we treat our enemy.'[5] It is here, in the mainstream of life, that the Christian must bear spiritual fruit. It is here, in the maelstrom of life, that Satan will blight our freedom. It is here, in the cut and thrust of twentieth-century living, that we must be conquered by God's Spirit.

For another of the Spirit's tasks is to equip and encourage us to defend our freedom. Paul was ever-conscious that the battle would be fierce.

## Fighting for freedom

Fighting for freedom means just that: conflict. But in Ephesians 6 Paul reminds us that we do not fight in our own strength. Rather, we are to clothe ourselves with the comprehensive equipment, the spiritual armour which is not unlike a Roman soldier's armour. This armour is provided for every Christian by the Holy Spirit.

The first thing we learn as we examine this armour is that it is designed to protect every part of our body except the back. We must therefore beware of the jelly-kneed whine which protests, 'I can't help myself, it's too big for me', when confronted with a choice between good and evil; the spinelessness which turns its back on obedience and exposes our vulnerability to the Evil One. Instead, in our quest for freedom we must equip ourselves with the resolve and strength the Holy Spirit offers in order that we may stand our ground, confront evil and fight to win. Jesus fought evil to the bitter end. We must do the same. Jesus is our model in this, as in everything.

We must equip ourselves with the strength the Holy Spirit offers. We have already noted that a number of meanings cluster under the Spirit's title of 'the Comforter': counsellor, helper, intercessor, advocate, strengthener and standby are some of the words translators use to describe the third person of the Trinity. The word 'to comfort' also means to exhort, to challenge, to encourage, to enable. It is military language. A rally-call. An encourager in battle would not merely *exhort* his troops to sally forth, he would pour courage into the faint-hearted and strength into the feeble. The encourager was a person with the insight and skill to enable a very ordinary soldier to cope gallantly with a nerve-fraying and risk-taking operation.

This is an essential part of the Holy Spirit's work. Thus he provides us with assurance of salvation, a protective helmet which is quite as protective as the leather and brass one the Roman soldier wore. He leads us into the truth. This truth, buckled around our waist, fulfils a two-fold function, just like the military belt. It holds all the other pieces of armour in place. It also provides a resting-place for the sword, that double-edged, defensive weapon which Jesus wielded so proficiently.

The Holy Spirit arms us with 'weapons of right-eousness in the right hand and in the left' (2 Corinthians 6:7). We must learn to be adept at wielding the sword of the Spirit. We must also learn skill in our handling of the shield: the faith in God for which men of all ages have been acclaimed, the faith which claims with Paul, 'I know whom I have believed, and am convinced that he is able to guard what I have entrusted to him . . .' (2 Timothy 1:12). This is the faith which brings God from the background of our lives and places him in sharp focus in the foreground. This is the shield which, like the Roman soldier's, extinguishes every lighted, pitch-soaked dart the Enemy chooses to hurl at us. This is the faith which prompts us to strap around ourselves the breastplate of righteousness, the bullet-proof vest which protects us where we are most vulnerable; the faith which is deepened as we receive the Spirit's weapon of prayer. This faith defends our freedom, prompting us to stand our ground even in the face of blistering temptation, encouraging us to go into battle fully armed.

Where the Spirit is, there is liberty. Much has been written about that liberty. In this chapter we have concentrated on the less well advertised, more discon-certing angles of the Spirit's liberating task. He

87

convinces us of personal sin. He purges, goads and purifies. But the hand which prunes is the hand which cultivates. The voice which convicts is the voice which enables. The heart which loves frees us to love. How does God free us to love as he loves? That is the subject of the next chapter.

## Notes for chapter five

[1] J. I. Packer, *Freedom, Authority and Scripture* (Inter-Varsity Press, 1982), p.46.
[2] Robert Frost, *Set My Spirit Free* (Logos, 1973), p.39.
[3] William Temple, quoted by John Stott, *Basic Christianity* (IVP, 1971), p.102.
[4] William Barclay, *John's Gospel: The Daily Study Bible* (Saint Andrew Press, 1955).
[5] Jim Wallis, *Call to Conversion* (Lion, 1981), p.10.

# 6

# *Free to love*

If we would become more like Jesus, we must learn to love. He is love. To love involves change. Indeed, change is the essence of sanctification. As Paul reminds us, the Spirit's work is to change us continuously so that eventually we are transformed into the likeness of Christ (2 Corinthians 3:18).

This inevitable change is both joyful and disconcerting. It is disconcerting because it introduces into our lives an unpredictability which perturbs some people. They prefer to hide behind a mask – 'This is the way I am. I cannot change.' As one man expressed it to me once, 'To change would be to leave the known for the unknown, to set sail on an uncharted sea.' For him, as for many of us, an unsatisfactory certainty, life as it was, seemed more secure than the promised certainty of a new and brighter life in Christ. For him, as for many of us, to begin to learn whole new patterns of loving was a daunting prospect.

Even so, the task of the Holy Spirit remains: to set us free truly to love. Until we love as Jesus loved, we are not free, but frozen. Until the love of Jesus is perfected in us, the love which is patient and kind, the love which is stripped of arrogance and me-centredness, we are neither free, Christ-like, nor mature. In this chapter, therefore, we must continue our pursuit of Christ-like freedom by considering three questions: Why do I find it hard to love? How might the Holy Spirit remove these obstacles in me? What is the goal I am striving to reach?

## Why do I find it hard to love?

Whole books have been written on the subject of love – about blockages, about the loneliness which stems from man's inability to give or receive love. There is space here to highlight just a few.

### *Childhood hurts*

Childhood impressions bite. Childhood hurts frequently lie at the root of a person's reluctance to reach out for love in adulthood; a person's fear of receiving love. It is not for nothing that the claim is sometimes made, 'Give me a child until he is seven, then you can do what you like with him.' The first seven years of life are the most formative years. Hurts caused then may leave a permanent scar and severely impede the love-learning process in later years.

Alice felt the draught of her love-less childhood well into adulthood: 'When I was a tiny little girl, I was put in an orphanage. I was not pretty at all, and no-one wanted me. But I can recall longing to be adopted and loved by a family as far back as I can remember. I thought about it day and night. But everything I did seemed to go wrong. I tried too hard to please everybody who came to look me over, and all I did was drive people away. Then one day the head of the orphanage told me a family was going to come and take me home with them. I was so excited, I jumped up and down and cried. The matron reminded me that I was on trial and that it might not be a permanent arrangement. But I just knew it would be. So I went with this family and started school in their town – a very happy little girl. And life began to open up for me, just a little.

'But one day, a few months later, I skipped home from school and ran in the front door of the big old house we lived in. No-one was at home, but there in the middle of the front hall was my battered old suitcase with my little coat thrown over it. As I stood there and looked at that suitcase, it slowly dawned on me what it meant . . . they didn't want me. And I hadn't even suspected . . . That happened to me seven times before I was thirteen years old.'[1]

A chill ran through my entire body as I copied out that story. Don't imagine that is an isolated tear-jerking incident. This kind of child-rejection is happening every hour of the day in the western world. Even in the middle of writing this chapter, a man came to me for help. During the course of the evening he said, 'I never ever felt loved by my parents. I've never really felt loved by anybody.' But like all adults, he cries out for love. And this is where the Holy Spirit moves in. He comes into devastated lives, like Alice's and this young man's. He gathers up the fragments of childhood hurts and pieces them together, remoulding you until you become the loving, lovable person he always intended you to be. The remoulding is not hurried, rarely instant. Most of us could not cope with a dramatic change in such a hyper-sensitive area. No. The Holy Spirit is a gentle, sensitive healer who knows how, when and where to apply his healing balm. He takes us by the hand and teaches us to trust in gentle stages. He teaches us to climb love's gradient by first taking us on the nursery slopes and only exposing us to the heights very much later on. We must learn to be as patient with ourselves as he is with us. After all, patience is one of the ingredients of love (1 Corinthians 13:4), therefore a prerequisite of freedom. While this learning is in progress, we may not feel at all free. But the exciting thing is that we are on the way to becoming free, more free than we have ever been before.

*The hurting adolescent*
Childhood hurts are not the only causes of frozen love, however. Hurts inflicted in adolescence are just as likely to cause us to cast our warmest emotions into the deep freeze and leave them there for preservation.

This was what happened to Simon. A home-loving, sensitive, creative child, Simon was devastated to discover at the age of eleven that his parents had decided to send him to boarding-school. 'Why?' was the question which burned inside him. 'What have I done wrong?' He dared not voice these questions lest his parents should think he was being insolent. So to boarding-school he went.

He hated it. He was the spotty bookworm, the introverted type, not the sporty kind of lad who won everyone's adulation. Every day he fought back the tears. Every day the river of sorrow inside him swelled.

Each holiday he tried to pluck up courage to ask his parents if he could become a day-boy. Each holiday his courage failed. Over the years, all ability to give and receive love was stifled. It was the only way a sensitive youth could pick his way along the pathway of a seemingly love-less life. Simon learnt to camouflage his hurt with a plastic smile. No-one suspected the fermenting anger which the smile concealed.

This adolescent love-deprivation continues to make serious inroads on Simon's ability to love, even though he is now in his late twenties. This is not surprising. As John Powell reminds us, 'The adolescent is especially sensitive to criticism and disparagement. He needs abundant affection, encouragement, praise and attention to counteract the demoralizing experiences of the class-room, the athletic field and the scramble for social acceptance.'[2] Accepting love was denied Simon. The Holy Spirit's task now is to thaw those frozen emotions so that Simon learns the lessons of love which could have been learnt in a loving environment.

At first Simon found the drip-by-drip thaw alarming. Then he realized what was happening to him and relaxed. From time to time situations arise which bring to the surface old and painful memories which were once repressed from necessity but, though buried, were very much alive. As these memories spring to the surface, Simon is discovering the joy of handing them over to God, not to indulge in harmful introversion, but to experience the health-giving peace which always pervades when pain is viewed from a God-ward perspective. The thaw is slow, steady, persistent, gentle, and often painful. But Simon's smile is no longer plastic. It is real. Little by little he is becoming more like Jesus — able to reach out to offer a rescuing hand to others, able to ask others for help, able to forgive his parents for the unintentional hurt they had inflicted. This is the beginning of wholeness, freedom.

## The hurting adult

If childhood pain scars and adolescent pain cripples, hurts inflicted on adults also sting. If we are honest and aware, we all know that love hurts. The choice which faces us as adults is to love and be hurt or not to love and suffer an indescribable loneliness. As Jim Bigelow puts it, 'We can either love and risk being hurt or not love and be sick.'[3] True as that may be, the hurts inflicted by those who say they love us cause us to yelp, to stand back from even wholesome relationships and to reevaluate our capacity and willingness for love. And our lives are blighted.

John Powell puts this well:

We know that if the bud of a flower is injured by hostile forces, like an unseasonal frost, it will not open. So, too, a human person who is without the warm encouragement of love, and who must endure the chilling absence of praise and affection, will remain closed in on himself. The dynamics of his personality will be jammed. And, if the dynamics of personality are seriously impeded, the result will be what psychologists call *neurosis*.[4]

As an Argus poster puts it, 'Only love can open and unfold the human flower.'

Into the frost-bitten, loveless places of our adulthood, the Holy Spirit comes teaching us love's art: to forgive the friend who inflicted the pain, to think more highly of the other's welfare, growth and happiness than our own, even to take responsibility for him, to safeguard *his* wholeness. This is true love. And if we would emulate Jesus, we must go on loving until it hurts. But how hard it is to love like this! There remains a gulf between our love-potential and our present realization of love. The Holy Spirit's subversive activity works to close the gap. This is necessary because we are only truly free when we can truly love. But the Spirit's work, though thorough, is gradual. This is another reason why we should be patient with ourselves and him while this pain-eradicating process is in progress. Let every sign of the Spirit's healing work be an encouragement. Let it remind us, too, of his promise: 'While we live in this earthly tent, we groan with a feeling of oppression; it is not that we want to get rid of our earthly body, but that we want to have the heavenly one put on over us, so that what is mortal will be transformed by life. God is the one who has prepared us for this change, and he gave us his Spirit as the guarantee of all that he has in store for us' (2 Corinthians 5:4–5, GNB). 'The Spirit is the guarantee that we shall receive what God has promised his people, and this assures us that God will give complete freedom to those who are his' (Ephesians 1:14, GNB).

## The stiff-upper-lip-syndrome

'God will give complete freedom' – the other side of eternity. Meanwhile we groan as we try to rid ourselves of hindrances like the stiff-upper-lip-syndrome, the kind of survival kit Simon was forced to wear at his boarding-school and one of the curses of British education. Jim Bigelow makes some scorching comments on the aloofness, the 'big boys don't cry', 'I-can-stand-on-my-own-two-feet' mentality, which the 'old school' demanded.

The stiff upper lip, with its requirement of individual strength, is an unbearable task master. It requires that we maintain self-control at all times and that we appear calm and unruffled on the outside no matter how much we may be troubled within. Thus, we develop masks to wear in various social settings to help us hide our fears, uncertainties and embarrassment.[5]

This manner of self-mastery was not modelled for us by Jesus. In Jesus there was not one shred of pretence. On the contrary, he expressed feelings through words, groans, tears and 'body language'. In John 13:21, we read that Jesus was openly 'troubled'. A few pages earlier, John takes us to the grave of Lazarus where we find Jesus weeping openly. 'Jesus wept' (John 11:35). And the reaction of the crowd? 'See how he loved him!' (John 11:36). It is John, too, who describes Jesus' physical fatigue – a weariness which Jesus made no attempt to conceal – 'Jesus, tired as he was from the journey, sat down by the well' (4:6).

Jesus was free to love because he was real. The Holy Spirit's task is to re-shape us so that we become less and less like the world, riddled with self-deceit, encumbered with masks to fit a variety of occasions, and more and more like Jesus: genuine, authentic, loving people. But it takes time, often years, to take the risk, to untie the masks, to be real. Even then, this side of eternity we shall not be as transparent as Jesus was. It also takes time to see through the hypocrisy of the super-spirituality which has been the diet many of us were fed with from the moment we turned to Christ.

*Short-sighted super-spirituality*

This short-sighted spirituality claims that we do not need others. We can go it alone. God is our refuge and strength. He alone is sufficient. Verses are extracted from the Bible to give weight to this erroneous claim. 'When you pray, go into your room, close the door and pray to your Father' (Matthew 6:6); 'I can do everything through him who gives me strength' (Philippians 4:13). But this emphasis is lop-sided. It is only one side of a two-sided coin. This isolationist, self-sufficient, over-spiritualized philosophy results in unutterable spiritual aloneness, even neurosis, and it was not modelled by Jesus.

Jesus' pattern was this. He spent hour after hour alone with his Father. 'Very early in the morning, while it was still dark, Jesus got up, left the house and went off to a solitary place, where he prayed' (Mark 1:35). 'He withdrew about a stone's throw beyond them, knelt down and prayed, "Father . . ."' (Luke 22:41). But into this indispensable God-sufficiency he wove inter-relatedness, fellowship. 'Jesus went out and saw a tax collector by the name of Levi sitting at his tax booth. "Follow me," Jesus said to him' (Luke 5:27). 'Jesus took Peter, John and James with him and went up onto a mountain to pray' (Luke 9:28).

Moreover, there were times when Jesus specifically asked to be supported. 'The sorrow in my heart is so great that it almost crushes me. Stay here and keep watch with me' (Matthew 26:38, GNB). If Jesus sought to be understood, loved and consoled, this cannot be

97

selfishness. It must be an important strand of fellowship. For many of us the Holy Spirit's biggest task is to turn the water of self-sufficiency into the wine of interdependence so that we see that interdependence and God-sufficiency complement and feed one another. Neither on its own is sufficient to meet all of our soul-needs. Together they carry us into freedom.

Our next task is to examine this aspect of the Spirit's liberating work, to focus on the goal we are striving to reach.

## The goal: to be like Jesus

The goal in this, as in everything, is to become more like Jesus. If Jesus presented us with a pattern of loving, this is the pattern on which we must cut our lives.

For me, personally, to see the value, the rightness and the Christ-likeness of asking for help from others has taken years of Holy Spirit intervention. Even two years ago, the fierce independence with which I prided myself and with which I had protected myself for years was deeply ingrained. It seemed a part of my nature. It also seemed desirable. I took as my motto the prayer of St Francis.

> Make me a channel of your peace . . .
> O Master, grant that I may never seek
> So much to be consoled as to console;
> To be understood as to understand;
> To be loved, as to love with all my soul.

And when my own heart ached, I would climb into my

ivory tower, pull up the drawbridge and find solace in God alone in private, interior prayer. It had never occurred to me that thus to safeguard my self-sufficiency was un-Christ-like.

The group of musicians God asked me to pastor became my teachers. Unknown to themselves, they became God's instruments in revealing to me the value of fellowship, the joy of belonging and the costly, yet healing art of being vulnerable. Through them I gained a biblical perspective. Through them I learnt that not only must I nurture my friendship with God but that, like Jesus, I must also value interdependence. For sinful man this involves allowing the Holy Spirit to remove, brick by brick if necessary, the walls of our separateness so that the twin goals, God-dependence and inter-dependence, may be reached.

## Man: born for relationship

The reason why we must be aware of our need for others is two-fold. First, because the Bible makes it plain that man was born for relationship, not for isolation. Second, because, as we have seen, Jesus modelled inter-relatedness.

The Bible gives us occasional glimpses of the relation-ship which existed between the Father, the Son and the Holy Spirit before the foundation of the world. John 17:5 is one example of this. Here we eavesdrop on a conversation between Jesus and his Father. 'And now, Father, glorify me in your presence with the glory I had with you before the world began.' John 1 is another example of this. 'Before the world was created, the Word already existed; he was with God, and he was the same as God . . . Through him God made all things; not one thing in all creation was made without him' (John 1:1, 3, GNB).

Before the beginning of creation relationship existed, a relationship between three co-equal persons which was characterized by co-operation, communication and two-dimensional love – giving love and reciprocal love.

Man was born in the image of God. 'Then God said, "Let us make man in our image, in our likeness" ' (Genesis 1:26). It follows, therefore, that man was born capable of and needing relationship.

Not only was he capable of interdependence, but we discover that even in Paradise an indescribable loneliness overwhelmed him when the opportunity for such fellowship was not provided. God's observation in Genesis 2:18 was a profound statement which modern man needs to etch on his very soul. 'It is not good for the man to be alone.' The deepest need in man is the need for relationship, to leave the condemned cell of his aloneness and discover a soul friend. This is so obvious, yet we fail to see it. Like Andy, we build our lives over our inner emptiness and project happiness to the watching world. But as Andy admitted to me, ' "Impoverished" is a good word to describe me. That's just what I am.' He went on to explain.

'I was driving home through the country lanes this evening and the sun was low in the sky, just peering through the trees. It was beautiful. And I thought back to last week when I was on a skiing holiday in the mountains. It was magic, you know. As we reached the top of one mountain, you could look ahead and see mile after mile of virgin snow. Not a single foot-mark marred it. It was wonderful. So much beauty. Such good health.

I've got a fulfilling job, too – in fact I have to tear myself away from it, I enjoy it so much. Yet some days I wake up and wonder, "Is this all life is?" And inside me there's an emptiness. I'm hollow, an empty shell. The dull ache gnaws away inside me and I wonder if I can live for another forty years carrying the burden of my aloneness.'

Andy's problem? He had never learnt to forge a close relationship. He did not know how to begin.

There is no need for us to remain clueless. Jesus not only pointed to the goal, he showed us how to reach it. He demonstrated how to create close relationships.

## Jesus' close relationships

Jesus began with an attitude, not with a person. Love is what Jesus is. It is a part of his essential personhood. It was the orientation of his will and personality. Therein lies our primary task. That is why the Holy Spirit whittles away at the hangovers of our past, healing us to set us free so that we become the loving beings God wanted us to be, so that love can pour from us in ever-widening circles, as it did from Jesus.

Love, outgoing love, was Jesus' reason for existing. This love was expressed in intimate ways to Peter, James and John. The ripples spread to include the Twelve. The crowd was not excluded from these circles of love, neither were the outcast: beggars, lepers, women. Jesus' love included everyone. This is our model. This is our goal. But where do we begin?

*Intimacy begins with prayer*
It would appear that Jesus selected his disciples on the

basis of prayer. We read that before calling the disciples he retreated to the hills for a whole night of communion with God. Did he ask the Father a specific question? 'Father, who are to be the men who will live and work with me?' The prayer, if he prayed it, is not recorded but we read that, immediately after that prayer-time, Jesus chose twelve men to be his disciples. He seemed to know whom he was looking for. Do we assume, then, that his Father had given specific instructions about this choice? Had the Father told him that Peter, James and John would give him special support?

If these assumptions are correct, is there an example here for those who find friendship a perplexing, elusive phenomenon, those who do not find that friendships just 'happen', those who find themselves caught up in unhelpful, even unhealthy relationships? Should we also ask a similar, specific question, 'Lord, I seem to have many acquaintances but few real friends. Whom have you chosen for me for friendship?'

### Commitment

Jesus' friendships were secure because he committed himself to them. After his nocturnal conversation with his Father, and having made the choice, he dedicated himself whole-heartedly to making the relationship work. As Jack Dominian[6] helpfully observes, Jesus' friendship reflected a warmth characterized by continuity, reliability, predictability and constancy. Jesus did not experiment with closeness and then withdraw; the fickleness that wounds in adult loving. No. If Jesus called you to be his friend, you knew exactly where you were. 'If I say I'll be your friend, I'll always be your friend.' The Holy Spirit's goal is to lead us to the point of personal freedom where we can love like that. First, our love for God must be a committed love. Next we need to ask God for a small group of close friends; three is a good number. Then, we should ask God for a bigger group of people who matter to us. From this wealth of love, given and received, we too are set free to love others; to offer supportive care to the needy.

## Closeness

Jesus was unafraid to express affection. His love was an intimate love. It was expressed through non-erotic touch: we find a woman of dubious reputation smothering him with tears and kisses (see Luke 7:36–38) and we see John leaning his head on Jesus' bosom at the Last Supper. These demonstrations of affection were warm, innocent, non-genital, but deep. If we would be like Jesus, at ease with our own sexual make-up, as he was, we must also learn the delicate art of appropriate touch.

'Touch? I've never touched anyone in my life!' This protestation from a thirty-year-old simply highlighted his need for healing. He was terrified of touch because he had never experienced the joy of demonstrative love during his childhood. As Jim Bigelow observes, 'Infants and children who grow up in a "non-touch" culture become adults with all manner of fears and hang-ups where affection and intimacy are concerned.'[7] Jesus had no such inhibitions and the Holy Spirit's work is to free us from ours: to free us *for* intimacy. It sometimes makes me sad that some Christians are not more free in this area. They cannot see that Jesus did not create us to be wooden-tops but warm, flesh and blood people like Jesus. They cannot see that woodenness restricts freedom.

Jesus' love was expressed, not only in touch, but also in looks and words. What did Peter see in the Lord's eyes in the court-yard on that unforgettable Friday? The Bible doesn't tell us. Could it have been hurt love, the pain a person feels when a dear friend has rejected him? What did the woman caught in the act of adultery see in Jesus' eyes? Again the Bible remains silent. Could it have been accepting love? What did Mary and John see in Jesus' eyes as he hung on the cross? Undoubtedly, tender, suffering but generous love.

The Bible is not silent about the ready way in which Jesus vocalized love. Take some verses from John's Gospel, for example. John 15:9 (GNB) reads, 'I love you'; John 15:12 repeats this, and John 13:34 says, 'I have loved you'. Jesus was unafraid to express affection. This expression of love is an expression of his richness, his aliveness. The Holy Spirit would similarly see us break out from the winter of lovelessness to the spring-time of love felt and love expressed. Thus we not only emulate Jesus but we feel ourselves growing up, maturing into the outgoing people he always intended that we should become.

As we have already noted, the willingness to be transformed into the image of God includes the willingness to increase our vulnerability as well as our strength. That is not to say we should bare our souls to everyone but it does imply that there should be two or three Christians with whom we can be completely maskless. This demands a humility and openness which does not find a ready niche in most of us. The Holy Spirit's activity will melt our natural reserve, if we are willing.

## Be filled with the Spirit

'If we are willing.' How do we give expression to that willingness to co-operate? I think this is included in Paul's injunction, 'Be filled with the Spirit' (Ephesians 5:18). To be filled with the Spirit means to be filled with God – no more, no less. To be filled with God means to be filled with love. God is love. This Spirit-filling is no optional extra for super-keen Christians. It is a requirement for all Christians. It is the way to reach our goal. What it entails, I believe, is this – you allow the fabric of your life to be held in the dye of his life until every fibre is tinged with his shade of love. There must be no attempt at tie-dying, the process whereby some patches of cloth are deliberately protected from the dye-stain. No. Every particle must submit itself to the penetrating influence of divine love. Every particle must be transformed. This dye keeps its colour best when the fabric is held in the vat daily. The Christian who exposes himself regularly to divine life, allowing it to be interwoven with his own, believing that God is at work within him, will find himself displaying Christ-like love: in word, touch, look, commitment, orientation and will. It may take years. It often does. But the miracle of love will happen. And the man who truly loves is truly free.

## Notes for chapter six

[1]Keith Miller, *Habitation of Dragons* (Word Books, 1970), pp. 185–186.

[2]John Powell, *Why Am I Afraid to Love?* (Argus, 1982), p. 92.

[3]Jim Bigelow, *Love Has Come Again* (Lakeland, 1978), p. 49.

[4]John Powell, pp. 27–28.  [5]Jim Bigelow, p. 43.

[6]Jack Dominian, *Cycles of Affirmation* (Darton, Longman and Todd, 1975).

[7]Jim Bigelow, p. 48.

# 7

# *Free to be human: free to be me*

In the last chapter, we observed some of the methods the Holy Spirit uses to free us to love as Jesus loved. In this chapter we continue our brief study of love-in-action, Jesus-style. It is an invitation to compare and contrast ourselves with him in our quest for Christ-like freedom. We also ask: How can I grow more like him? How can I become more like the genuine, maskless person he was? How might the Holy Spirit begin to untie my many masks: false humility, self-inflation, the pseudo-self I project to the world? Then in the next chapter, we investigate another problem: How might God heal my insecurities and handle my pride?

First, we examine the masklessness of Jesus, the only mould which should shape our lives.

## The genuineness of Jesus' life

The first love-ingredient we observe in Jesus is the genuineness of his life. A man's genuineness is proved by his concern for others. Jesus was the man for others.

He demonstrated this concern in a wide variety of ways.

*Jesus affirmed people*

One of the finest qualities of Jesus' self-donating love was his ability to affirm those with whom he rubbed shoulders. Think of his affirmation of Simon Peter, a mere fisherman. 'Jesus said to Simon, "Don't be afraid; from now on you will catch men" ' (Luke 5:10). Or think of his affirmation of the Canaanite woman whose daughter was demon-possessed: 'Woman, you have great faith!' (Matthew 15:28). After an encounter with Jesus, a person came away strengthened. That is what 'to affirm' means: to make strong, to draw out another's full potential, to reinforce all that is good.

*Jesus took responsibility for people*

Another attractive facet of Jesus-love is his load-bearing care for others. He protected those he loved. He took responsibility for their emotional, psychological and practical needs. He met those needs with sensitivity, skill and non-possessive, non-smothering affection.

We see this beautifully enacted in those gruelling hours leading up to the Last Supper. With painstaking care, Jesus prepared his friends for the pain of bereavement they were soon to suffer. 'Do not let your hearts be troubled . . . In my Father's house are many rooms; if it were not so, I would have told you. I am going there to prepare a place for you. And if I go and prepare a place for you, I will come back and take you to be with me that you also may be where I am' (John 14:1–3).

This self-giving love which detected and ministered to the inner needs of the loved one was in evidence after the resurrection also. Think of Mary weeping at the empty tomb. Jesus saw. He cared. He came. With one economical, power-filled word he consoled her, 'Mary' (John 20:16). Or think of Thomas. Into the empty shell of his doubt, the risen Lord came with the much-needed invitation, 'Put your finger here; see my hands. Reach out your hand and put it into my side. Stop doubting and believe' (John 20:27).

*Jesus forgave*

Jesus set people free by forgiving their doubts as well as their failures. He refrained from humiliating them or rejecting their desire to make amends. Even though he felt the sting of rejection as keenly as anyone else, the strength of his love was such that it mattered more to him what happened to his friend than what happened to himself. This is a superlative quality of loving.

## Jesus revealed his own limitations

But perhaps the most startling ingredient of Jesus' love was the ease with which he revealed both personal strengths and personal limitations.

On the cross, in his moment of greatest vulnerability, strength poured out of him to his heart-broken mother and his equally desolate friend. 'When Jesus saw his mother there, and the disciple whom he loved standing near by, he said to his mother, "Dear woman, here is your son," and to the disciple, "Here is your mother" ' (John 19:26–27).

Yet there were moments of unashamed limitation: the pain-stricken walk to Calvary, the helplessness of infancy. There were other limitations, too. Thus when

James and John made their request of preferential treatment in the kingdom, Jesus replied, 'I do not have the right to choose who will sit at my right and my left. It is God who will give these places to those for whom he has prepared them' (Mark 10:40, GNB). Jesus was a man under authority, a man in submission, a man with set limits, yet he was gloriously free.

What was the secret of his transparency? What kind of person is it who detects the strengths in others and affirms them? What kind of person is it who is more concerned for the welfare of the loved one than his own well-being? What kind of person is it who readily forgives? What kind of person is it who has no need to project a pseudo-self; who clearly states what his limitations are?

The person who loves in this way enjoys a double security. He is secure in the love of God and therefore secure in his God-given identity. Moreover, he has the capacity to see himself as God sees him, as a child of the Father. In other words, he has learnt the difficult art of self-acceptance. Like Jesus, he can even accept his humanity.

## Self-acceptance

The challenge which faces us if we would be free in Christ is to love as Jesus loved. As we have seen, the prerequisite of such love is self-acceptance. We have to learn to accept ourselves in the same way as Jesus accepted himself, acknowledging both personal strengths and personal limitations. Until we do this we have only a weak, watered-down love to offer to others.

Herein lies a problem. None of us crossed the

threshold into the overlap with an innate ability to value himself as much as God values him, see himself as God sees him, or really esteem himself as a child of God. Indeed, many of us suffer from such a poor self-image that we fail to see any good in ourselves at all. Therefore each Christian is required to learn this difficult art. The Holy Spirit, the liberator, faces a gargantuan task as he seeks to deliver us from the distorted view of ourselves we may have lived with since childhood, so that we are free to view ourselves as God sees us and hear and feel the love with which he loves us.

Certain obstacles barricade the path to this inner freedom. These must be removed before the way is clear for us to enjoy the spaciousness of the inner freedom Jesus enjoyed. Here there is space to consider just two of these obstacles: childhood messages and crippling comparisons.

As we saw in an earlier chapter, messages implanted in our mind in childhood produce prolific growth well into adulthood. The effect is often as problematic as the suckers which have sprung up all over my lawn recently. And the treatment is the same. The tap-root must be traced and dealt with. Until this happens in the human heart, our self-picture remains at best distorted, at worst grotesque, as Gill found.

Gill was an inquisitive little girl. Like many children, she frequently tuned in to adult conversation, was quick to absorb facts but slow to interpret them accurately. This sometimes resulted in distress. Gill vividly remembers one such occasion when she was six years old.

Her doctor, a friend of the family, had just been giving Gill a thorough medical examination. While Gill was dressing, the doctor turned to her mother and said, in a casual, jocular way, 'Of course, you realize Gill will never be a teacher or anything like that? She's not clever enough.'

A casual remark? It was a remark which wormed its way into Gill's heart and, until a few months ago, twenty-year-old Gill still lived within its limitations, so that whenever anyone invited her to take a position of responsibility at work or at church, she would giggle nervously and brush them aside. 'Oh! Thank you ever so much for inviting me. But I couldn't do anything like that – I'm not good enough.' It was as though Gill's memory resembled the hall of mirrors at a fair. Whenever she gazed into any of those mirrors, the person staring back at her was grossly misshapen, not fully integrated, someone to mock.

This warped self-picture resulted in serious spiritual paralysis, for although Gill's mind registered what the Bible has to say about every child of God, her emotions refused to receive this teaching. The old tape, 'You're not clever, you're inadequate,' still played so loudly that it drowned the still, small voice of God whispering within.

In the next chapter we shall see how the Holy Spirit of God intervened in Gill's life enabling her to turn away from the distorted image; enabling her to begin the adventure of self-acceptance.

## Crippling comparisons

The reason why some Christians loathe themselves even more than they hate the spider which runs over their bare feet in summer has nothing to do with external circumstances. Rather, the reason lies within themselves. Take Ruth, for example.

111

When I first met Ruth, I was attracted immediately by her bright smile, her trendy, baggy trousers, colourful sweater and contrasting head-scarf. I liked this expression of her creativity. But it soon became apparent that what attracted me, repelled her. Ruth put it dramatically. 'Do you know how I see myself? I'll tell you. I think I'm really disgusting. Yes. That's it. Disgusting. I'm like a filthy beggar sitting in a corner not even daring to lift up the empty bowl of my life for God to fill.'

Ruth went on to explain the reason why these feelings of self-loathing had eaten into her in the same way as dry rot spreads into the fabric of an old building.

'It's my sister. She's pretty – and clever. Her 'A' levels were brilliant. *She* got into university. But look at me. All I'm good for is studying art. I've always compared myself with my big sister. I look at her face – she really is lovely – then I look in the mirror and I say to myself, "You're ugly. Really ugly." And I know I'm second-rate.

'Then there's my granny. She was a really lovely lady; always neat, well-dressed, well-spoken. I thought I should be like her. But look at me. I mean – I'm not a bit like that. I'm just a slum. How can I believe all the good things God says about me when I'm like this?'

When, like Ruth, we have spent twenty years or more comparing ourselves unfavourably with others, it is as though we filter everything anyone says, including God. If someone compliments us, we spiritualize it, 'Oh! It wasn't me. It was the Lord.'

The tragedy is that in filtering everyone's affirmation, withholding it from the inner recesses of our being, we never assimilate the truth about ourselves. The truth about myself has nothing to do with how I see myself, how I feel about myself or how I rate in comparison with others. The truth about myself, the secret of my identity, rests in God. It is vital, therefore, if blockages like the ones we have been considering are to be removed, that we explore certain questions in a thoroughly objective way: How does God see me? What does he say about me? Is my thinking in line with his?

## Search the Scriptures

The first thing we must do if we are to answer those questions accurately is to search the Scriptures and extract from them the priceless treasures contained there. As we apply ourselves to this task, some interesting and maybe unexpected facts emerge.

One is that the Bible nowhere teaches that self must be completely obliterated. Since pride is at the centre of sin, Jesus called his disciples to *deny* self, to take up their cross, to follow (see Mark 8:34). He also taught that the seed must die before it can grow and that his followers must donate all they have and are to him (see John 12:23–26). But for too long Christians have misunderstood these exhortations.

Jesus did not mean that we should be snuffed out like a flame or sucked into the total mass of Christians to become like a drop of water that loses itself in a bucketful. He came to give us life and to give it abundantly (see John 10:10). And when Paul uses the picture of the Body of Christ he does not mean that each of us becomes an anonymous blood-vessel or identical hair. On the contrary, each of us is specifically called to be different, individual, valued. Each of us has a unique contribution to make to one another and to God (see

Romans 12: 1–8). And each of us is uniquely loved.

That is why some Christians encourage us to love ourselves and underline that such self-love is both good and necessary. Unfortunately, this phrase can be misleading. In other contexts, 'self-love' means self-centredness, pride, self-satisfaction, the very things the Lord came to save us from.

When the Bible talks of self-love, and incidentally, it *assumes* that we will love ourselves, it means that we value ourselves sufficiently to look after ourselves by attending to our needs: physical, psychological, spiritual, emotional (though not necessarily giving in to our wants – see Matthew 25:35–39; Ephesians 5:33). It means we accept ourselves as a vital part of the Body of Christ (1 Corinthians 12–14), that we do not belittle our worth before God. It also means that, like the Psalmist, we marvel at ourselves as a part of the wonder of God's creation (Psalm 139:13–14), that we hold ourselves in high esteem because we were created in God's image (Genesis 1:27) and have been redeemed by the death of God's son (Galatians 6:14). It is in these things that we glory. And this is the sense in which we love ourselves.

Christians who fail to love themselves in this way live impoverished lives. The words 'God loves you' seem to mock rather than console. Such people are filled with an inner pain which prevents them reaching out to others. It is imperative, therefore, that we learn to accept ourselves.

In order to do this, we must delve into the Bible's pages to discover what God says about our worth as unique human beings. Then we must realize, take on board, God's assessment of us. We must assimilate

God's view of us, each of us a person who matters to him. The Bible underlines time and time again that God loves us, desires our highest good and has placed such a high value on us that he sent his very own Son to redeem us (see John 3:16; 15:9; Romans 5:8; 1 Peter 5:7; Revelation 1:5).

## God's child

The Bible makes it clear that we are not just a valuable asset for the extension of God's kingdom. Our value is even higher than that. We, who have committed our lives to Jesus, have become God's children. We in the West take this so much for granted. A young friend of mine who was recently converted from Buddhism helped me to see the immense privilege which is ours. 'I don't know if you can imagine how it feels, after years and years of worshipping idols out of fear and duty, suddenly to know that you are loved – loved by Almighty God, your heavenly Father.'

John helps us to drink in the wonder of this fact. 'How great is the love the Father has lavished on us, that we should be called children of God! And that is what we are! . . . Dear friends, now we are children of God' (1 John 3:1–2).

Children are living expressions of their parents' love, the focus of their providing care, the people in whom is their chief delight. This is what we are (see Ephesians 1:6; Philippians 4:19). In the eyes of God we are somebody. And Jesus assures us that our heavenly Father knows how to give *good* things (see Matthew 7:11).

## You are God's masterpiece

The Bible goes even further. Paul implies this in Ephesians 2:10, 'We are God's work of art' (JB). Each of us is a mini-masterpiece, an essential contribution to the whole. In the same way as every word is vital to a powerful poem, every flower and leaf essential in a flower arrangement, every stroke of the brush necessary in a great work of art, so each of us is unique, an original, without exact replica, irreplaceable.

How this jeans-wearing generation needs to absorb this vital message! Before the living God you are not just one of the crowd, never lost in a sea of anonymity. Before the living God you are special. You are his unique design; a design which cannot be repeated. As John Powell puts it, 'After God made you, he broke the mold.'[1]

It is easy to know this with our heads but to reject it in our behaviour. So we find students wishing they could become like their pastor or the president of the Christian Union. Or we find young men and women aping well-known Christian leaders, like the young man I met recently whose voice as he gave a book review was a near-accurate take-off of a very well-known preacher's.

But God did not bring this student into the world to become a cardboard cut-out. Neither does God want you to become a carbon-copy of anyone other than his Son, Jesus Christ (see Romans 8:29). Your way of giving expression to the Christ-like image cannot be reproduced by anyone else. You are an essential piece of God's vast jigsaw, or, to put it another way, a unique part of that mysterious Body God delights to label, 'The Bride of Christ'.

## You are God's friend

Jesus himself made it clear that he desires our friendship (see John 15:15). Read those words again slowly.
Drink in the implications. The Son of God has chosen
you to be his friend, with all that that means in terms of
caring, sharing and intimacy. Jim Packer helps us to
understand the full depths of this breath-taking
statement.

There is tremendous relief in knowing that His love
to me is utterly realistic, based at every point on prior
knowledge of the worst about me, so that no discovery
now can disillusion Him about me, in the way I am so
often disillusioned about myself, can quench His
determination to bless me. There is certainly great
cause for humility in the thought that He sees all the
twisted things about me that my fellow-men do not
see (and I am glad!) and that He sees more corruption
in me than that which I see in myself (which, in all
conscience is enough). There is, however, equally
great incentive to worship and love God in the
thought that, for some unfathomable reason, He
wants me as His friend, and desires to be my friend,
and has given His Son to die for me in order to realize
this purpose.[2]

The above is only a fraction of the Bible's teaching
which persuades us to value ourselves. Believe it. Allow
it to turn your own view of yourself inside out, especially
if you are one of those Christians who have somehow
been .beguiled into believing that self-belittling is a
virtue, a sign of true Christian humility. And if, like Gill

and Ruth whom I mentioned earlier, you are among those who have been programmed by parents, teachers, friends, your inner self or Satan's lying tongue, to despair of yourself so that the Bible's teaching sounds reassuring for everyone but you, then do not close this book in desperation. Turn instead to the next chapter and ask God whether the ministry I describe there might be one of his ways of helping you over the next hurdle and beyond into the pathway of freedom. And, as I have already underlined, make prayer a priority. We all need this miracle-working closeness of God's presence.

## Keep close to Jesus

The disciples were not unlike many of us: insecure, mask-wearing, highly motivated, yet failing. Like Christians today, they quarrelled, competed with each other and camouflaged their uncertainties as best they could. But a touching scene in the musical *Godspell* suggests that, as the earthly ministry of Jesus drew to its close, the disciples' need to hide their true identity began to disappear.

Many Christians, myself included, were disturbed by the portrayal of the person of Jesus in this particular musical. But the scene I refer to was a powerful one. It is the Last Supper. Jesus has washed his disciples' feet. He prepares for the final farewells. He moves around the table, embracing, kissing or playfully ruffling the hair of one disciple after another. Then he does a curious thing. He holds up a mirror in front of each disciple in turn and, as he does so, the disciple is seen removing his make-up. Why? In the presence of Jesus, you can afford to untie your masks. In the presence of Jesus you can afford to be real.

Jesus had loved these men through three action-packed years. What need was there now for camouflage? Jesus had revealed and reinforced each man's residual strength and potential for good. Then what was there to hide? In the company of Jesus, life-changing miracles had taken place. The disciples had begun to see themselves as Jesus viewed them: loved and lovable, accepted and acceptable. Friends.

What Jesus did for the disciples, he wants to do for us. That is one reason why prayer and Bible reading are so important. A person cannot understand himself, accept himself or value himself until he has been understood, loved and accepted by another. As we saw in the last chapter, we are not proficient at loving one another. The only person capable of giving us one hundred per cent acceptance is God. Become rooted in him and all the ingredients for self-acceptance are at your disposal.

## Be tamed

This is not to say that other Christians have a small role to play. On the contrary. The significant thing about the *Godspell* scene I described is that no disciple removed his own make-up. He looked in the mirror while he allowed another to wipe his face clean. And that is much more costly. Costly, but vital. If we are to take the risk and untie our masks, we must be lured out of the false security of our mask-wearing by the reassurance of an accepting and understanding person or group of people. No-one has demonstrated this to me more vividly than Chris.

When Chris first came to see me, he was one of the loneliest people I have ever encountered. He was in his late twenties but had only ever experienced even a modicum of closeness with one other person in his entire life. This friend, a flat-mate, had just moved, leaving Chris bereft. The pain of separation seemed unbearable.

When he came to see me, he gave voice to his feelings of loss and bereavement. We invited God to come into the lonely void. And we looked at Chris's circle of acquaintances. Where could he, a single, shy, introverted person, find security, warmth and a place of belonging? He doubted whether he could take the risk of taking the initiative and making new friends.

I happened to know of a church in the town where Chris lives and suggested he tried it.

Three months later, he visited me again. I scarcely recognized him. His eyes were shining. He smiled. He was full of news about his fulfilling job and the new church.

'Chris. You're so different. What's happened?'

In answer to my question, he laughed. 'It's the house group at that church you told me to go to. The services on Sunday aren't at all what I'm used to. But the house group is great. They were pleased to see me – welcomed me. They look out for me at church. They're friendly. They even seem to appreciate me. I feel wanted, accepted. I didn't know it could be like this.'

The members of that house group are probably totally unaware that they have been instruments of God's healing for Chris. They conveyed to him a message we all need to hear: 'I am lovable! I don't have to do anything or be anything but myself. I am worthwhile in myself.'[3] It often takes others to convey that soul-soothing message, as John Powell points out. 'I need your love and you need mine. I need to see my worth and beauty in the reflection of your eyes, in the sound of your voice, in the touch of your hand. And you need to see your worth mirrored back to you by me in the same way. We can succeed or fail together, but separate and alone we can only fail.'[4]

It's not only that we need each other, but as Christians we are actually a part of one another. Paul emphasizes this in his letter to the Christians in Corinth: 'Now the body is not made up of one part but of many' (see 1 Corinthians 12:14). As we saw in the last chapter, a vital component of Christian freedom is interdependence within the Body. Before we can enjoy this freedom, however, the Spirit of God has to chip away at the raw material of our lives like a sculptor chipping away at a piece of marble. Broken trust patterns, hurts, angularities, have to be dealt with in us just as the eccentricities and insecurities of other members of the group have to be discarded. This takes time and patience. We need to be tamed. Like the fox in Antoine de Saint-Exupéry's charming story, *The Little Prince*, until we are tamed, we do not know how to belong.

### The tie which frees

Perhaps you know the moving scene where the fox invites the little Prince to tame him?

'Come and play with me,' proposed the little prince, 'I'm so unhappy.'

'I cannot play with you,' the fox said, 'I am not tamed.'

'What does that mean – tame?'

'It is an act too often neglected,' said the fox. 'It means to establish ties.'

'To establish ties?'

'Just that,' said the fox. 'To me, you are still nothing more than a little boy who is just like a hundred thousand other little boys. And I have no need of you. And you, on your part, have no need of me. To you, I am nothing more than a fox like a hundred thousand other foxes. But if you tame me, then we shall need each other. To me, you will be unique in all the world. To you I shall be unique in all the world . . .'

'What must I do, to tame you?' asked the little prince.

'You must be very patient,' replied the fox. 'First you will sit down at a little distance from me – like that – in the grass. I shall look at you out of the corner of my eye, and you will say nothing . . . But you will sit a little closer to me, every day . . .'

The next day the prince came back. . . . So the little prince tamed the fox.[5]

When someone loves you, tames you, takes responsibility for you, that person sets you free to be human, free to be the unique person God always intended that you should become, free, even, to love yourself in the same way as Jesus loved himself.

If we would know this freedom we must allow the Bible's teaching to stamp us with its own design. We must spend time with God and spend time being tamed by others, allowing ourselves to be loved, allowing ourselves to be accepted, allowing ourselves to be praised. We must recognize that just as love was Jesus' mission, so also it is ours. We must therefore submit to this three-fold vocation: to love God, to love ourselves, to love others.

A person who is at home with himself as Jesus was, a person who glories in his uniqueness as Jesus did, a person who can echo the Psalmist's words, 'I thank you . . . for the wonder of myself' (Psalm 139:14, JB), is on course for freedom.

But maybe you are not there? Maybe you harbour hatred in your heart against God or life for not making you someone else, for giving you the wrong-coloured hair or the wrong-shaped nose? Maybe you hammer the doors of heaven in your anger: Why do others receive all the flamboyant gifts? Why not me?

There is no future in this futile fighting. Forgive God. Forgive life. Forgive yourself. And accept yourself as you are because God accepts you as you are, loves you as you are and commands you to do the same (see Romans 5:8; Colossians 2:16–23). In this acceptance lies peace and the freedom to be 'fully human, fully alive'.[6]


## Free to be human

The fully human, fully alive person is the best advertisement there is for Christianity. He is most like Jesus. Yet the world laments, and rightly, that many Christians seem spineless, 'wet', anaemic, or so intensely spiritual that they have lost sight of life as a celebration.

Jesus' life was far from colourless or joyless. He promised us not merely life but superabundant life. 'I have come in order that you might have life – life in all its fullness' (John 10:10, GNB).

For Jesus, living fully entailed appreciating the grandeur of the world around him. 'Look at the lilies . . . look at the birds.' It meant appreciating people: the widow with her copper coins (Luke 21:1–4); children playing in the market-place, even the prostitute's adoration (Matthew 26:6ff.). It included an appreciation of solitude, 'He went out of the town to a lonely place, where he prayed' (Mark 1:35). And it caused him to identify with the intensest light and deepest shade of human emotion: yearning (Matthew 23:37), sorrow (John 11:35), wonder, awe, tenderness and ecstasy.

The Holy Spirit's work in us is a transforming work: to change us into the likeness of Jesus. The God who 'richly provides us with everything for our enjoyment' (1 Timothy 6:17) would have us appreciate the beauty of creation just as his Son did. He who has entrusted us with talents: creativity, music, art, dance, to mention a few, would have us unfold into freedom by expressing ourselves through these gifts. An essential part of Christian freedom is this: at last, I am free to be me; the me Jesus always intended that I should become.

## Notes for chapter seven

[1] John Powell, *Why Am I Afraid to Love?* (Argus, 1982), p.24.
[2] J. I. Packer, *Knowing God* (Hodder and Stoughton, 1973), p.41.
[3] John Powell, *The Secret of Staying in Love* (Argus, 1974), p.19.
[4] John Powell, *The Secret of Staying in Love*, p.32.
[5] Antoine de Saint-Exupéry, *The Little Prince* (Piccolo, 1982), pp. 66–70.
[6] John Powell, *Why Am I Afraid to Love?*, p.24.

# 8

# *Emotionally free*

In chapter two we observed that, when we were born again, we did not arrive as new-born babes in heaven itself. We were born into the overlap, the country which lies between the old and the new. We reflected that this middle-world is often a place of tension, conflict, struggle and pain. It is as though we were born on the holy mountain where God dwells, but we arrived at the foot of the mountain, not the top. We now have a climb to make.

We have examined some of the ways God equips us for the journey. We have established that our eventual success is guaranteed. We have also seen that there is no human mould into which we must squeeze ourselves. Our aim is to become the person Jesus always intended we should be and to be transformed into his likeness.

In the last chapter we pinpointed some of the reasons why even highly-motivated Christians find the pathway to wholeness blocked, find themselves unable to discern the voice of God, find themselves paralysed instead of gladly adventuring into obedience. In this chapter we go on to consider some of the ways God might remedy these situations and thus deliver us from insecurities and fears.

One of the ways God both prepares and equips us for freedom, enabling us to realize our full potential, is to serve us. For proud, self-sufficient, modern man, this is sometimes a bitter pill to swallow. It is true nevertheless. And necessary.

You may protest, 'Surely, I am here to serve God?' Yes, you are. But it very often happens that the legacy we bring into the overlap – failure, hurts, bondages – prevents us from serving God in the way he wants to use us. Before he can set us to work, he has to do *in* us what he wants to do *through* us. Take Peter, for example.

Jesus was not blind to Peter's potential. One day he affirmed the strengths he saw. He called Peter, 'The Rock'.

Peter? A rock? That is scarcely the word one would have used to describe him in the garden of Gethsemane where he was so overwhelmed with tiredness that he failed to support Jesus in his moment of deepest agony. It is scarcely the word one would have chosen to describe the one who stood warming himself by the fire later that night, who three times denied all knowledge of Jesus. It is scarcely the word to sum up the character of the despondent figure in John 21:3, the one who felt the strong pull of the old life and went fishing.

Put yourself in Peter's shoes. Wouldn't you be sick at heart if, in your mind's eye, in the small hours of the morning you had watched the action replay of the last hours of Jesus' life and seen yourself neglecting, denying and running away from the one you were supposed to love so fervently? Wouldn't you despise yourself as you reflected on your own extravagant assertion, 'Lord, I am ready to go with you to prison and to death' (Luke 22:33) and compared that glad promise with the sickening fall?

This is the legacy Peter brought into the overlap. And John goes to considerable trouble to demonstrate what happens when Christians in the overlap fail. After the failure comes the restoration.

Peter was to be instrumental in establishing the infant church. He was to set the captives free; to give sight to the spiritually blind. But how could he begin to fulfil this ministry while he was in bondage to his own failure?

And Jesus saw. Jesus came. Jesus cared. Jesus restored. He did *in* Peter what he would later do *through* him.

The resurrected Jesus came to Peter on the beach in the cool of the morning and asked a simple but profound question. 'Simon, son of John, do you truly love me . . .?' (John 21:15).

Was it necessary for Jesus to ask this question? Was it not obvious that from the moment Peter spotted his master there on the tiny beach, the love which sprang to life in him was warm, tender and emotional? Yet Jesus did ask the question – three times.

'Do you truly love me?'

'Do you truly love me?'

'Do you love me?'

Why did Jesus persist? Was it because he knew that as Peter heard himself repeat the reply, 'You know that I love you.. . . You know that I love you.. . . You know that I love you. . .', healing would come to his grazed and battered spirit; the horror of the memories of that irreversible denial would be touched? Or was Jesus concerned that after the ascension Peter's lingering memory should be the sound of his own voice resounding with confident and affirming love rather than the hollow echo of those empty, fear-filled lies. We can only speculate and use our imagination creatively to re-enact that early morning scene. But what John makes crystal clear is that *after* Peter's restoration comes his re-commissioning, 'Feed my sheep.'

Think for a moment of the full implication of this re-instatement. Before Peter's restoration there was no way he could feed the flock of Christ. His resources were depleted. But now, having been cared for by Christ and ministered to by him, he could carry this tenderness, restorative love and healing to others. And the good news for us today is that just as Jesus delighted to use Peter, so he still delights to use wounded healers.

Some branches of the Christian church are in danger of losing sight of this biblical principle which Paul highlights in 2 Corinthians 1.

## The principle of spiritual overflow

'Praise be to the God and Father of our Lord Jesus Christ, the Father of compassion and the God of all comfort, who comforts us in all our troubles, so that we can comfort those in any trouble with the comfort we ourselves have received from God. For just as the sufferings of Christ flow over into our lives, so also through Christ our comfort overflows' (2 Corinthians 1:3–5). The principle of spiritual overflow operates in this way: Jesus meets me in my need so that I can meet others in their need. It does not mean that I am above the need for personal ministry and always have at my fingertips the resources to serve others. That is spiritual pride and foolishness. It is also unbiblical.

In speaking of this overflow, was Paul thinking back to the Damascus Road, his blindness and God's ministry to him through Ananias? Or was he recalling other occasions when God met his specific needs through other Christians? We are not told what precisely was in Paul's mind as he wrote. We do know that this was a principle which featured greatly in his own life and ministry.

This principle of the overflow highlights the quality of life in the overlap. It demonstrates that the overlap is the place where acceptance, love, understanding, affirmation and a sense of belonging abound. It illustrates that the overlap is the place where each person has status and a purpose in life. Acceptance, affirmation, status, security? But these are the ingredients essential for a person's growth. And that is what the overlap is: the place where we gradually shed the legacy of the past and grow into the emotionally free, mature persons God always intended that we should become. As we have seen, his methods of bringing us into maturity are gentle and incisive. His insight is perfect. Only he knows where to apply his restorative love.


## Rescue from obsessional sin

This restorative love is unfailing. This gave hope to Tim when a shadow stole over him and he confessed to finding life in the overlap perplexing and painful.

Tim told me his story. From childhood he had been on the receiving end of teasing from boys at school. Tim was a sensitive child and the hurtful nicknames had wounded him more than anyone recognized.

In his early teens, the names and the insecurity gave birth to the fear that he had homosexual tendencies. In an attempt to discover for himself whether this was true or false, he began to buy girlie magazines. His interest became obsessional and resulted in sexual fantasy, experimentation with fetishes, and an ever-increasing conviction that he was gay.

Then Tim met Christ. For five years he grew as a Christian. He became a person of stature and integrity. His knowledge of the Bible was enviable, his prayer-life challenged many of his friends and God began to use his creative gifts in powerful ways. And then it happened. The desire to fantasize re-appeared. The girlie magazines at the back of the cupboard seemed to weave a spell around him again. The need to masturbate seemed compulsive. Tim was disgusted with himself; deeply ashamed.

For five years he had considered himself to be free from lust. Now the legacy of the past which he had brought into the overlap had raised its ugly head again. Tim felt trapped and a hypocrite. How could he serve God with this secret pressing in on him?

This dilemma is not rare. The old habits and appetites you bring into the overlap seem to be in submission for a while. Then it is as though they receive an injection of new energy. They rise up and assert themselves. There are many reasons for this.

Although we live in the overlap, we are still human.

In the overlap we live in the world, we live with the desires of the flesh and we co-exist with the devil. Neither sin nor the world, the flesh nor the devil was eliminated when we set out on the journey from the old world into the new. We live in the middle-world. We have easy access to our old life-style. We have easy access to the compulsive desires within us. And the devil has easy access to us. We may have renounced the world, the flesh and the devil, but they have not renounced us. Therefore the climb to the mountain peak will be arduous at times. The difference is that whereas in the past there was no chance of survival, now our eventual victory is guaranteed. We may have access to the past, sin may have access to us, but we also have access to God through the Holy Spirit and he has access to us.

The reason why God sometimes allows us to fall into the kind of trough Tim was in is three-fold. First, he wants to cut us free from specific sins which, like cling-foil, seem to cover us with a second skin. Second, he wants to educate us so that we may more effectively move towards the new life-goals he gave us when we were born again. Third, he wants to set us emotionally free by restoring an accurate self-image, as we shall see later. Thus the crises of our lives become growth crises, the pathway to increased freedom.

## Growth crises

Sometimes, of course, these growth crises can be dealt with in a straightforward way. I think of a young man who came to see me recently. Among the string of problems we discussed was lying. Whenever he finds himself in a tight corner, he tells lies to cover up his failure. Of course, one lie leads to another and he frequently finds himself steeped in deceit. I challenged him to resolve to live biblically – words which he took very seriously. The next day in his Bible reading, these words seemed to shout from the page: 'Rid yourselves of all malice and all deceit' (1 Peter 2:1). God's Word jolted him into action and he is now enjoying adventuring into obedience, telling the truth in small things as well as big.

Or I think of a young mother whose spiritual growth was being hindered by her attitude to one of her children. 'She's so demanding and I find myself eaten up with resentment against her sometimes. She seems like an intrusion, not a gift from God.' As this woman repented of her attitude and as we prayed, a purging seemed to take place. A few weeks later, she told me: 'All the resentment has gone. It's as though my love for her has been completely restored.'

It very often happens that this kind of prayer and counsel enables a person to take a big step forward on the pathway to freedom. But when counselling Christians in need it is not uncommon to come across those for whom the balm of this kind of ministry is ineffective. For years, like others in the counselling ministry, I puzzled over this until I discovered a different dimension of prayer ministry which some people call 'inner healing'.

You will not find this healing process spelt out in the Bible, just as you will not find plastic surgery described there nor ministry to depressives or alcoholics. What we do find in the Bible are the general principles which lie at the root of this ministry. Let me describe two examples of inner healing and then link them back to biblical principles.

## Tim

I have introduced Tim into this chapter already. God used the ministry of inner healing to set him free from the sin of lust which had gained a firm foothold in his life.

The reason why Tim seemed incapable of breaking free from the tyranny of lust was that a childhood opinion of himself, 'I'm not normal', had lodged in his mind and dominated his thinking and behaviour. Neither seemingly relevant Bible verses, nor praying with him in the way I have described so far could dislodge this crippling self-loathing. It seemed necessary, therefore, to invite Tim to go back in his imagination to the playground at school where that message was first implanted and to ask God to heal the hurts which had been inflicted during that phase of his life.

In prayer, using his imagination, Tim relived some of the playground incidents I have mentioned, re-owning the boyhood feelings as he did so. As we reconstructed the events as they had actually happened, Tim could hear his playmates' taunts as clearly as ever. He began to weep.

I invited him to look around the playground to see if Jesus was anywhere present. Gradually Tim became aware that Jesus was there and with this new realization in his mind, he began to talk to him. 'Is it true what they're saying about me, Lord?'

As though in answer to that question, Jesus seemed to take Tim on a journey through adolescence and adulthood. He gave Tim clear indications that his sexual orientation was heterosexual, not homosexual. The signs had been there all the time but Tim had failed to see them because fear of homosexuality had bound and blinded him. It was as though Jesus held up a mirror. Tim looked and saw himself loved and touched and held within the love of God – in a love which extended right back to his childhood.

I remember the occasion well: the relief, the joy and Tim's quiet wonder as he experienced God's compassion for him personally.

A week later, I met Tim again. Now that he was free from that message which had mocked him for more than twenty years, he readily forgave the boys who had scarred him emotionally. He also repented – turned his back on – the lust which had dogged him for so many years. This readiness to forgive those who have deliberately or unwittingly caused the hurts of the past, together with the need to accept full responsibility for and repent of any ensuing sin, are essential steps to the freedom Tim went on to enjoy: freedom to believe that what the Bible says about every Christian applies to him, as to every child of God, freedom to obey God's commands. That is not to say he never fantasized again or that he gained instant perfection. He had learnt to enjoy sin. Now he is learning that to say 'No' to self-gratification and 'Yes' to God is a discipline which floods him with a mysterious, all-pervading joy.

In telling Tim's story, I am not making a general comment on homosexuality. Nor am I wishing to imply that the climb out of the gay life-style, even for the committed Christian, is easy. It is often long and arduous, accompanied by loneliness and struggle, but it is possible.

The reason why Jesus was able to set Tim emotionally free was that he was willing to co-operate. Tim wanted to change. Where this desire is absent, no change is effected. God does not force wholeness on to us. But where that desire is present, God is ever ready to work on the raw material of our lives. His clay-wet hands will continually remould us until finally we shall be conformed into the likeness of his Son; our ultimate goal, and his.

## Gill

Gill, whom I introduced into the last chapter, was also in bondage to one of Satan's lies, a lie which came to her at the age of six through her doctor: 'Gill will never be a teacher or anything like that. She's not clever enough.'

This lie was unexpectedly exposed when I invited Gill to become a Sunday School teacher. Gill refused. But some time later she reopened the conversation. 'You know, I don't understand myself. I really love children, as you know. I think they're really lovely. But when you asked me to be a Sunday School teacher recently, I panicked. "I couldn't. Oh! I couldn't," I said to myself. "Think of all the responsibility." But there's another part of me that knows I *could* do it. And that makes me really cross with myself. I really want Jesus to set me free from whatever it is that's holding me back so that I can serve him like I want to.'

When we prayed together, asking God to expose the source of the feelings of inferiority, lifting the lid off Gill's past, the old memory of the doctor's surgery sprang into Gill's mind.

I invited her to return, in prayerful imagination, to the doctor's surgery, to become the little girl again, dressing and eavesdropping, and to hear again those damning words, 'Gill's not clever.'

'Yes. I'm there. I can see it all clearly and hear him saying it.'

We then went on to ask God to reveal to us what his assessment was of Gill.

In the silence which followed, a verse of Scripture came into my mind; some words from Isaiah which applied first to Israel, but which have meaning for every child of God. 'Fear not, for I have redeemed you; . . . since you are precious and honoured in my sight, and because I love you. . . . Do not be afraid, for I am with you. . . .' (Isaiah 43:1, 4–5); 'You will be like a beautiful crown for the LORD. No longer will you be called "Forsaken" . . . Your new name will be "God is pleased with her" . . . Because the LORD is pleased with you' (Isaiah 62:3–4; GNB).

As I read these promises aloud, I heard Gill gasp. She told me what had been happening to her in the silence. In her mind's eye she had seen a picture of a huge hand, which she took to be the hand of God, holding a precious stone, a jewel, which he seemed to assure her was herself. The picture and this Bible passage slotted together and seemed to be God's answer to our prayer, 'Show us how you feel about Gill.' The message was liberating. From that moment the doctor's assessment of Gill lost its power.

Over the months, Gill assimilated more and more of the Bible's teaching about her own worth before God. Slowly she gained in confidence. When I last saw her, now thriving on Christian leadership, her cheerful comment was, 'It's as if I've suddenly grown up. It's great.'

## Prayer ministry

It is important that we consider what this ministry is and what it is not.

This prayer ministry has nothing to do with changing the circumstances of the past. The past is past. What has happened has happened and cannot be changed. Neither is this ministry wishful thinking or the breaking of a spell, like the kiss of Prince Charming which sets the princess free.

No. In this ministry, we realize the Lordship of Jesus, not only of the present and the future but also of our entire past; we invite the Holy Spirit to anoint the hurts of the past with the truth of the written Word or the soothing presence of the living Word; we spread before God the chaos of personal sin, pain or confusion and ask him, by the power of the brooding Spirit, to create cosmos out of chaos. And we look for his healing, reconciling, bondage-breaking touch.

I have emphasized that the past is past and cannot be changed, that Tim's playmates can never be silenced, that Gill's doctor's assessment of her cannot be erased. No. Inner healing cannot reverse circumstances. What it can do, and does, is to remove the sting from the memory so that the memory loses all power to hinder a person's present growth.

This is what happened for both Tim and Gill. There was a time when Tim dared not recall his unhappy childhood. It was too full of haunting memories. Now it is as though the cellar of his life has received an overdue spring-clean. It is a place where Tim can roam with ease because he knows that it comes under the Lordship of Jesus who has cancelled out its power to inhibit.

Similarly, Gill can now laugh about her doctor's remarks. Jesus, through prayer, removed the sting so that the memory has no hold over Gill's growth.

Some Christians believe that the lack of reference in the Bible to this particular form of ministry invalidates it. Surely, they argue, if Jesus wanted us to work in this way he would have used the method himself to model it to us? In my view this is a blinkered approach to the healing, liberating work of the Spirit of God. The Bible nowhere describes major surgery, but we submit to the surgeon's scalpel and medicine's healing when occasion demands. It is my personal view that to invite a person in pain to re-live and re-own the past so that past hurts nestle under the shadow of Christ's healing wings instead of being left raw and exposed to the harshness of a brash world is not unbiblical but Christ-like in its compassion. Neither is it unbiblical to believe that the Holy Spirit longs to anoint the weeping wounds within with the soothing oil of God's truth; longs to bind up broken relationships, restore and rebuild. This is his work. To apply it today is thoroughly consistent with the Bible's teaching. When you see for yourself the fruits of this liberating activity of the Holy Spirit, you can only marvel at the goodness and gentle power of a healing God.

## To whom can we go?

It will be obvious from what I have written that I believe that for some Christians the ministry of inner healing is the missing key for which they have searched long and hard. But to whom can such people go to receive help?

This ministry demands time, skill, prayerfulness and

God-dependency. It is a serious matter, in the name of Christ, to seek to come alongside another's pain and to alleviate it. This ministry must not therefore be trifled with, nor played with like a toy. But God is investing the necessary gifts in his church. If, therefore, at some stage in your life, God seems to show you this could bring you over a hurdle, seek the help of your pastor or an experienced counsellor. Ask them to put you in touch with someone who can help you in this way if they, too, feel this is the best next step for you.

There are many popular books on the market which describe in detail how certain techniques have worked in certain situations and there are many speakers who describe, in a moving way, their own particular method of ministry. Some books and speakers are more biblical than others. Don't swallow all you read or hear on this subject and beware of jumping on the inner-healing band-wagon. Don't seek ministry because it is the 'in thing' to do. No. If, like Tim or Gill you find yourself in a spiritual cul-de-sac and God seems to prod you, go to someone you know and trust, if possible, someone who also knows you. That is why I suggest your own pastor or vicar.

I sometimes look at the congregation I know best: St Nicholas' Church, Nottingham. There I see hundreds of individuals. Some seem so well-adjusted, capable. They appear to cope with life in the overlap without anyone's help but God's. I talk to others: some with emotional hang-ups, some with sexual scars, some with a variety of hangovers, and it underlines, for me, the fact that we are all different; unique. God will therefore meet us in different and unique ways. He has many ways of bringing each of us into increased freedom.

I don't know why some people march through the overlap enjoying one degree of freedom after another. I don't know why others need to have his love applied to specific sins and specific wounds. What I do know is that Jesus wants to set each of us emotionally free. I also know that the words of a certain poster apply to me: 'Please be patient with me. God hasn't finished with me yet.'

# 9

# *Free from self*

Brokenness precedes freedom. The egg shell cracks open to set free the chick. The acorn husk disintegrates to let out the seedling oak. The nymph's body tears to release the dragon-fly.

This is not merely a principle of nature but a biblical concept also. Death precedes new life. The crucifixion anticipated the resurrection. As Jesus put it, 'A grain of wheat remains no more than a single grain unless it is dropped into the ground and dies. If it does die, then it produces many grains. Whoever loves his own life will lose it; whoever hates his own life in this world will keep it for life eternal' (John 12:24–25, GNB).

Doesn't this contradict everything that was pinpointed in the last two chapters? Isn't Jesus here commanding us not to accept ourselves but rather to reject ourselves? Self-denial certainly comes into Jesus' injunction but, as we saw in an earlier chapter, it is essential that we recognize that self-denial is reached in two stages. The first stage is self-acceptance. The second stage is self-denial. A person who has not learnt to accept himself cannot deny himself. The step is too big, too painful, too unreasonable.

We observed in chapter seven that self-acceptance was an intrinsic part of Jesus' life; Jesus was a man in perfect harmony with himself, God, others and the world. 'I am who I am' (Exodus 3:14). 'I and the Father are one' (John 10:30). For this reason, love flowed from him in ever-widening circles. We observed that, without certain ingredients, freedom ceases to exist. Among other things I must accept myself as the person God made me to be, accept the qualifications God has given me, accept the limitations he has placed upon me, accept the framework within which he allows me to grow.

In this chapter we must build on this foundation by asking some penetrating questions. If self-acceptance and self-denial are essential to discipleship, what is the me which must be carefully laid on one side; denied? If brokenness is essential to freedom, how might God proceed to break me? What is the end product? Do I become a nonentity, God's robot?

## Self-denial

My body is not a husk, a shell or an acorn, dying when the real 'me' is born. It remains a necessary part of me and it does not change. My height remains the same at conversion as it did before, the shape of my face does not change, the colour of my eyes does not change. Neither does my essential personality. If I was a creative person before I became a Christian, I shall continue to express myself in similar ways – probably more so. If I was an extrovert before, it is unlikely that I shall suddenly experience the swings of mood experienced by the introvert.

No. What must disintegrate is that dimension of my personality which Paul calls 'the flesh', our 'lower nature', as J. B. Phillips helpfully translates it. Everything in me which is polluted, which actively opposes the Spirit's revolutionary activity, which not only refuses to walk in step with God but which seems, at times, like a devilish tyrant demanding that I should deliberately disobey God, all this must die. The activity within, which sometimes causes me to wonder whether Satan has gained a bigger foothold in my life than God, must be dealt a death-blow.

Sin, with its resulting evil, was incubating in our personality from the moment we were conceived. Like the lethal disease, AIDS, it wastes the personalities God created for wholeness; it breaks down our immunity and leaves us spiritually weak so that we fall prey to the multiple infections of sin. When we wake up to the fact that we are helpless victims of this disease, we ask, 'What can I do to arrest the decay?' The answer is that we can do nothing to rescue ourselves from certain spiritual death.

When we commit ourselves to God through Jesus, he gives us his Holy Spirit who permeates our personalities, who is the antitoxin which counteracts this infection ravaging our entire being. Thus, when we are born again, we not only live *in* the overlap, there is an overlap living in us: the overlap of good and evil.

Paul describes how this conflict between good and evil rages inside us: 'For the sinful nature desires what is contrary to the Spirit, and the Spirit what is contrary to the sinful nature. They are in conflict with each other, so that you do not do what you want' (Galatians 5:17).

Paul admits, humbly and powerfully, that this state of affairs sometimes plunged him into near despair. 'In my mind I am God's willing servant, but in my own nature I am bound fast, as I say, to the law of sin and death. It is an agonizing situation, and who on earth can set me free from the clutches of my own sinful nature?' (Romans 7:22–24, Phillips). The answer? 'There *is* a way out through Jesus Christ our Lord.'

Through Jesus, with his help and the Holy Spirit's intervention, Paul persuades us, 'Put to death, therefore, whatever belongs to your earthly nature: sexual immorality, impurity, lust, evil desires and greed . . . anger, rage, malice, slander and filthy language . . . Do not lie' (Colossians 3:5–9). This is what must die so that the life of Christ may not be choked. This is what must die so that, day by day, our lives may more nearly resemble the life of Jesus. This is one of the meanings of self-denial; denying the sin in oneself the freedom to rule the roost, denying oneself the sick pleasure sin affords.

If this dying is to take place, two things must happen. First, we must accept ourselves as we really are: a conglomeration of good and evil, daring to accept that lust is as much a part of me as of my brother, that the seeds of pride and greed and envy germinate and flower as much in my life as in my brother's. Second, we must co-operate with the indwelling Spirit of God when he goads us and equips us to deal the death-blow to the enemy within. If we fail in the first of these duties, we remain eternally blind to the real situation, that imperfections in my life are marring God's image and putting the brake on my growth in holiness. If we fail in the second, we fall prey to the twin sins of quenching and grieving the Holy Spirit of God.

The Holy Spirit's work is to transform us into the likeness of Christ. Some of us cherish pet sins: fantasies, pride, jealousy, ambition, and so on. When we refuse to surrender these to the Spirit's disease-destroying activity, we grieve the Spirit. Whenever we neglect to listen to his quiet prompting, 'Surrender all', we quench him. By thus refusing to deny ourselves, we restrict the Spirit's effectiveness and weaken our own immunity to sin and temptation. Conversely, whenever we obey, however reluctantly, however tentatively, we co-operate with the Holy Spirit in bringing every particle of our sin-infected old nature into captivity so that the new life, Jesus' life, might grow up in its place.

'To transform us into the likeness of Christ.' This is the Spirit's goal. Our next task is to examine how this transformation might come about; to ask, 'How *does* God persuade me to submit myself to the Spirit's liberating, cleansing, healing activity?' Or, to use a biblical picture, how does he ensure that I respond to his knock, open the door of the rooms of my inner life, and invite him into every area of my life (see Revelation 3:20)? How does he break and rebuild?

## Broken through temptation

One way is through temptation. God allows us to be tempted so that we are brought face to face with the weakness or the evil which hides in the shadows of our hearts. This confrontation need not become the devil's trump card. It can be a learning situation. When Jesus was tempted in the wilderness he demonstrated how temptation can be converted to become a school for self-denial, the place where we learn how to use inner conflict creatively so that it pushes us into growth in holiness, growth in inner freedom. We examine the temptations of Jesus to observe how this worked in his situation.

Of course, there is a sense in which the temptations of Jesus do not find a parallel in our own lives. Jesus was sinless. No evil hid in him. But there is a very real sense in which he teaches us by example how to deal with Satan's subtle ploys so that God can bring us back from the temptation-ridden desert more full of the Holy Spirit's energizing than ever before.

What was Satan offering Jesus during his forty-day grilling in the desert? What was on offer was ample opportunity for self-gratification (bread would replace stones), self-fulfilment ('I will give you all this power and all this wealth', Luke 4:6, GNB) and self-glorification ('Throw yourself from the Temple. God will keep you safe. It will hit the headlines for miles around'). The nub of the temptation was this. Jesus was faced with a choice: to allow the driving force of his life to be self or God. He chose God.

Satan employs one temptation only: the temptation to rate self-gratification more highly than God-pleasing; the temptation to enthrone self and dethrone God; the temptation to substitute self for God as the top priority of our life. This temptation comes wearing many faces and a variety of disguises. But it is the same temptation. The way we handle it affects every choice we make.

A young mother is tempted to believe the feminist cry, 'You must discover yourself. Never mind about your marriage, your husband, your children.' A wealthy bachelor is tempted to furnish his new home with costly carpets and priceless antiques. 'Never mind that Christians in the Third World are starving; that our missionaries on furlough are feeling inflation's pinch.' A young man is tempted to make sexual conquests. 'Never mind that I am trivializing the sacred sex act; abusing another's body.' Temptation comes in many disguises. The root is the same: the temptation to make self supreme. Jesus renounced all claim to selfish ambition at the outset of his ministry.

When we emulate Jesus and decide before God that we, too, will have God as Lord, he may allow us to be sorely tempted so that that resolve may be strengthened. Every time we endorse our heart decision to make Jesus Lord, every time we resist the temptation to put self first, sin's stranglehold is weakened. Temptation then becomes the gateway to triumph; the place where the healing Holy Spirit races to rescue us from that intruding disease: self.

## Holy Spirit infiltration

When the Holy Spirit races to the rescue, like red blood corpuscles fighting an infection, something deep and irrevocable begins to take place. God transforms on a level which is inaccessible to reason and intellect alone. We begin to discover what inner freedom means. This Holy Spirit infiltration makes us more free, more integrated, more whole. He reaches our innermost thoughts and desires, brings about a gradual harmonization of the conscious and the subconscious so that we yearn, like Jesus, to choose God and not the dictates of self.

Was this, I wonder, what God promised through Ezekiel? 'I will give you a new heart and a new mind. I will take away your stubborn heart of stone and give you an obedient heart. I will put my spirit in you and I will see to it that you follow my laws and keep all the commands I have given you . . . You will be my people, and I will be your God' (Ezekiel 36:26–28, GNB).

A people who think God-thoughts, a people who love as God loves, an obedient people; these are a free people. This freedom does not come all at once, as we have seen. It comes piecemeal. This the way I see it. When we turn to Christ, he gives us his Holy Spirit, like a droplet of oil on the fabric of our lives. Little by little the drop of oil seeps into every fibre of the fabric, softening it, transforming it, breaking through the barriers. This is God's gentle way of breaking us. It is the disintegration of one life so that another, a richer, may come into existence. But we have to be willing, we have to give our 'Yes' to this emancipation and where we are as yet unwilling, we need to pray that the Spirit of God will make us willing to be made willing.

## Disappointments and trials

Just as God uses temptation, so he uses life's trials to persuade us to deny self and surrender to him.

It is said of Mahatma Gandhi that the direction of his life changed when travelling on a train in South Africa when he was twenty-four years old. At the time he was working as a lawyer. He boarded the overnight train with a first-class ticket.

At Maritzburg, a white man jumped on board. He

looked at Gandhi and went to the two railroad officers to complain. They tried to force Gandhi to leave the first-class compartment, but he showed them his ticket and refused to move. At the next stop Gandhi was thrown off the train and dumped onto the station platform. Years later, Gandhi was asked by a missionary, "What has been the most creative experience in your life?" Gandhi related this incident at Maritzburg. Here this Indian's life was re-directed. Within him was born the desire to fight the ugliness of colour prejudice with the weapons of love and non-violent resistance.[1]

Gandhi was insulted because his face was brown, not white. Peter warns that we may suffer insults because we are followers of Christ (see 1 Peter 4:4). Indeed, sometimes God allows disappointments, insults, pain, suffering of all kinds to re-direct our lives. These afflictions could be your most creative moment when the life of the Spirit breaks through the 'prison of your selfhood', to use Thomas Merton's phrase.

## Co-operating with God

How can we ensure that we use temptation and difficulties creatively? This was the question Andrew presented me with shortly after his marriage to Jo. 'Jo and I have been married for three months. At first we sat on cloud nine. It was marvellous. But now I look back on our three months together and I can't help thinking that the only thing it's taught me is how unbearably selfish I am. I love Jo but I criticize her if she burns the toast. I love her but I don't want to pray with her.

Personal prayer is far more important to me than together-prayer. I love her yet there are times when I want to be away from her. I want . . . I want . . . I want . . . Can you *hear* how self-centred I am?'

I could hear. And I reflected that another of the gentle ways God uses to break this absorption with self is to give us a partner or a friend to love intimately. Marriage and the intimacy of friendship very quickly highlight how much ground the Holy Spirit has yet to conquer in our lives. Marriage is therefore 'a means of grace'.

But to return to the question, How can Andrew ensure that marital problems result in a creative self-denial, not an ongoing battle to assert self? How can we ensure that the trials God allows us to undergo become similarly life-enriching?

One way to grow through problems is this. Make a note of the incident, either in writing or in your head. Reflect on your instinctive response and try to assess the implications. Then take the whole affair to God and ask him to inspire your thinking, to bring it into line with his, even if it means standing your own values on their head. Perhaps it would be helpful to apply those four points to Andrew:

| | |
|---|---|
| *Incident* | It is breakfast-time. Jo has burnt the toast again – the third time this week. |
| *Instinctive response* | Andrew is irritated. There is an angry outburst. Jo is upset, hurt and tearful. This ugly scene spoils yet another day. |
| *Implications* | Andrew is more concerned |

about *his* stomach, *his* need for a trouble-free breakfast, *his* need to be served, than his wife's sensitive feelings. Conclusion: he is innately selfish.

Jesus said, 'Love one another as I have loved you.' Jesus' love forgives, re-instates. 'Love is patient, love is kind . . . It is not rude, it is not self-seeking, it is not easily angered, it keeps no record of wrongs . . .' (1 Corinthians 13:4).

*Inspiration*

Moreover, love challenges me to break the obsession I have with myself. Love demands that I no longer live in a world of one. Love demands that I donate myself to others.

Looked at through God's perspective, a burnt piece of toast could become the turning-point of Andrew's life and certainly of his marriage if he would pray a prayer along these lines. 'Lord, you see my sin-infested self. Please perforate the protective layers which keep your Spirit far removed from this compartment of my life. Flow into me. Change me.' God delights to respond to that kind of prayer. Was it the kind of prayer which Paul prayed regularly? We are not told. What we do know is that the day came when God had so transformed Paul that he could make this astonishing claim, 'I no longer live, but Christ lives in me' (Galatians 2:20). It is as we learn to ask the question, 'Lord, how do you want *me* to change?' that we creep nearer to this enviable state.

## A lost identity?

Does this mean, then, that the Christian's true personality is gradually obliterated, that he becomes nothing more than a robot in the hand of God?

Not at all. On the contrary, the Christian who is allowing the Spirit of God to touch and transform everything in his world experiences an entirely new dimension of personal integration, wholeness and freedom. As one girl expressed it to me once, 'I feel like a flower which is gradually unfolding to the warm rays of the sun.' This girl was more truly herself than she had ever been before. It is always the way. The more you give of yourself to God, the more you become the person he created you to be. You become gloriously human, increasingly free.

The Holy Spirit will never erase your personality, never rub out the real you. Rather, he will perform his unseen work in the depths of your personality; and just as yeast makes the dough real dough, the dough from which bread and buns are made, so the Holy Spirit will make you – you. There will always be a glorious intertwining of your personality and his, as Paul assures us. 'God's Spirit joins himself to our spirits' (Romans 8:16, GNB).

We see all of this beautifully enacted in the transformation God effected in Peter.

Before Pentecost, Peter was the insufferable, self-assertive extrovert. At the transfiguration, it was Peter who blurted out, ' "Rabbi, it is good for us to be here! Let us put up three shelters – one for you, one for Moses and one for Elijah." (He did not know what to say, they were so frightened)' (Mark 9:5–6). At the Last

Supper it was Peter who swore his life-long allegiance to Jesus, 'Lord, I am ready to go with you to prison and to death' (Luke 22:33). This empty claim was followed closely by his impetuous attack on Malchus in the Garden of Gethsemane. 'Simon Peter, who had a sword, drew it and struck the high priest's servant, cutting off his right ear' (John 18:10).

After Pentecost, we read, 'Then Peter stood up with the Eleven, raised his voice and addressed the crowd' (Acts 2:14). After Pentecost, we find Peter exercising a healing ministry. 'Then Peter said, "Silver or gold I do not have, but what I have I give you. In the name of Jesus Christ of Nazareth, walk!" Taking him by the right hand, he helped him up, and instantly the man's feet and ankles became strong. He jumped to his feet and began to walk' (Acts 3:6–8). After Pentecost, Peter becomes such a charismatic figure that '. . . people brought the sick into the streets and laid them on beds and mats so that at least Peter's shadow might fall on some of them as he passed by' (Acts 5:15).

What has happened? How has this radical change come about? It is as though the old Peter has died and a new Peter has emerged; new, yet the same. The same, but manifestly different.

C. S. Lewis describes the nature of the change superbly. This change is required of all Christians.

Christ says "Give me *all*. I don't want so much of your money and so much of your work: I want *you*. I have not come to torment your natural self, but to kill it. No half-measures are any good. I don't want to cut off a branch here and a branch there, I want to have the whole tree down. Hand over the natural self . . . and I will give you a new self instead. In fact I will give you *myself*: my own will shall become yours."[2]

Deep down, isn't that what we want? Deep down, don't we all want at last to be able to claim with Paul that it is no longer the self-centred I which controls my life, but Christ?

## Stripping off the layers

But you may well ask, 'Isn't this loss of self painful?' At times, yes. At other times changes take place without your noticing.

While I was writing the last chapter, a blanket of fog settled in the valley in Derbyshire where I have come away to write. For three days, I looked out of my window and saw nothing but smoke-grey mist. On the third day, while I was gazing out of the same window, wondering how to introduce this chapter, the ghostly invader retreated, first to the valley below, then to the hills beyond, until he seemed to make a final leap over the horizon. Gone. I could see my view again: the clumps of purple heather in my neighbour's garden, the row of beech trees standing sentinel over the valley, the moors which tower above the gorge.

Deep inside us, the Holy Spirit is uniting with our spirit, making us into the children of God, transforming us into the likeness of Christ. Much of the time this transfiguration is hidden in the swirling mists of our self-centredness. So that the world may see, not us, but the living Christ in us, this illusory, projected self has to be swept away. Often its going is as silent and unexpected as the retreating fog..

At other times it is more painful, more dramatic. Like my treatment of the pine staircase in this cottage where I am staying. The cottage is over one hundred years old. Year after year, different owners have painted the staircase. One day I looked at the chipped paint on the banister and began to scrape away at it with my fingernail. 'When this cottage was built, they would have used *good* wood,' I thought to myself. 'Those chipped layers of paint probably conceal something very beautiful.'

I'm not a do-it-yourself person, but I bought some wonder-working paint stripper and applied it. It was magic. The paint of years fell away. Underneath lay a handsome, knotted pine banister. Its beauty had been camouflaged, completely hidden.

When God applies his paint-stripper to our lives, it can feel alarming . The reason why he allows you to undergo all manner of testing is that he detects the unique beauty which is a part of you; the beauty of your personality shot through with his Holy Spirit. This is what he wants you to see. This is what he wants the church to see. This is what he wants the world to see. And this is why he takes the trouble to remove the layers of your pseudo-self. It is why he asks you to deny yourself, to say no to all that is not Christ-like. When all that is not of him is laid on one side, cast away, all that is of him will be exhibited in its full glory.

C. S. Lewis put this persuasively;

It's only the Christians who have any idea of how human souls can be taken into the life of God and yet remain themselves — in fact, be very much more themselves than they were before . . . it is when I turn to Christ, when I give myself up to His Personality,

that I first begin to have a real personality of my own
. . . Look for yourself, and you will find in the long
run only hatred, loneliness, despair, rage, and decay.
But look for Christ and you will find Him and with
Him everything else thrown in.[3]

In Christ, my identity is not lost but mysteriously re-
discovered.

## Notes for chapter nine

[1]Keith Miller, *Habitation of Dragons* (Word Books, 1970), p. 28.
[2]C. S. Lewis, *Beyond Personality* (Bles, 1945), p. 41.
[3]C. S. Lewis, p. 15 and p. 45.

# 10

# *Free to sin?*

A choice confronts modern man, as every man: to lust, that is, to gratify self; or to love, that is to donate himself to God for others. In the last two chapters we have observed that the only people who are truly free are those who truly love, those who are being rescued from the bondage of self.

In this chapter, we place the spotlight on sin. To be more accurate, we focus on the good news that the Christian, the person who is 'in Christ', has no more need to sin. Why then *do* we Christians commit sin? What happens when the Christian sins? Can a Christian be restored to fellowship with God after he has deliberately, blatantly or unwittingly sinned? If so, does it really matter that we slip up from time to time? If God so delights to forgive, surely the more we sin, the more opportunities we give him to demonstrate his over-flowing, forgiving love?

These are the questions which will occupy our minds in this chapter.

## No need to sin

Christians today, I find, may be divided into two camps. There are those who are ever-eager to hear the good news, 'You do not have to sin. You can tackle temptation in this way.' To speak to such individuals or groups is heart-warming. They surely bring joy to the heart of God. 'There is . . . rejoicing in heaven over one sinner who repents' (Luke 15:7).

This almost continual state of repentance is not experienced by the other camp, however. Caught up in a spiral of defeat, they become discouraged if not rebellious. In the Preface of this book I referred to some known to me. One was Ron.

Sin held Ron as though by suction. Even years after he had become a Christian he seemed totally unable to extricate himself from the promiscuous pattern of behaviour which had first swept him off his feet in his mid-teens. On one occasion he described the force of its pull: 'I feel as if I'm in the grip of a power outside myself, which is greater than me and which takes hold of me. I am helpless in its grip.'

The good news which applies to Ron, as to all other Christians tormented by the strength of the sin which seems to hold them in a vice-like grip, is this: the seeming strength is superficial. Jesus' sacrifice on Calvary dealt a death-blow to Satan's power. Sin therefore has no more power over us. This is the objective truth which Paul proclaims in Romans 6. 'For we know that our old self was crucified with him so that the body of sin might be rendered powerless, that we should no longer be slaves to sin. . . . In the same way, count yourselves dead to sin but alive to God in Christ Jesus. . . . For sin shall not be your master, because you are not under law, but under grace' (Romans 6:6, 11, 14).

Whenever God asks us to do something for him, he equips us for the task. He would not call us to this kind of, seemingly impossible, objective living if he was unprepared to grant the wherewithal to obey. The strength to obey, even in the face of scorching temptation, is there. 'And God is faithful; he will not let you be tempted beyond what you can bear. But when you are tempted, he will also provide a way out so that you can stand up under it' (1 Corinthians 10:13). Why, then, do we fail?

## Why do Christians sin?

There is space here to consider only two reasons. First, because the sights, smells and sounds of the old country resurrect cherished memories. Second, because, in our stubbornness, we think we know better than God.

### Attraction of old habits

In chapter two of this book, we saw that when we turned to Christ, we did not travel out of the Land of Sin into the Land of Perfection. We journeyed into Middle-world; the Land of In-Between, the overlap. We saw that the overlap is the place where sin is still rife, where Satan rampages, where good and evil co-exist. We are like refugees trying to leave behind one culture in order to adopt another. We may be highly motivated. Even so, the habits of a lifetime are not discarded overnight. An Indian family has helped me to understand what this means.

This family was evicted from Uganda when Amin's

government cleared that country of Ugandan Asians. They have lived in Britain for ten years now. Yet on the rare occasions when they meet as a family, they eat traditional Indian food and they eat with their fingers: 'We like it that way. Somehow the food tastes better when taken with the fingers.'

I am not implying that a knife and fork is more hygienic than fingers. I am suggesting that habits die hard. Passions, for example, are slow to die. Ron, whom I mentioned earlier, put the situation powerfully. 'I can't begin to describe the suffering that is involved in crucifying a passion or trying to. A crucified passion, like a crucified man, is a long time dying and it dies hard and painfully.'

God understands the problem. He is patient with us. We must not fall into the trap of being harder on ourselves than God is. If we say yes to him, he will come alongside us while we learn that that dying passion, though it might beckon, though it might call, no longer controls us. Even though it reaches out to claw us, there is no power in its grasp. Our feelings may not readily assent to this fact but it is a fact nonetheless, to be reckoned with, experimented with and enjoyed. As Paul reminds us, 'It is God's will that you should be holy' (1 Thessalonians 4:3).

*Stubbornness*

'If we say yes to him, he will come alongside us.' The problem with many of us is that we refuse to say yes to God even when we most need him. Again, this is a hangover of the past. We enjoy running our own lives, making our own decisions. If anyone else dares to suggest an alternative life-style, we rebel, even if that 'someone' is a gadget.

We changed our car recently. This new model boasts an economy gear. There is even a gadget fitted into the dash-board which indicates how many miles per gallon the car is doing. A yellow light winks when the car decides the driver should change gear for the sake of economy. This little yellow eye irritates me intensely. I know it is irrational but there are times when I would like to speak to it quite firmly. 'Look here! I've been driving cars for over twenty years. I don't need you to give me the wink every time I should change gear. I'm well able to make my own decisions.' Some of us bring that sort of intransigence into our relationship with God. When the light of his Word reminds us to change gear, we rebel. We might even deliberately go against the light's advice and commit sins.

## What happens when we sin?

What happens if, like a girl I was talking to recently, we commit adultery, or blatantly commit some other form of disobedience against God? What are the consequences of opposing God? That question must be considered in two halves: What are the consequences for God? What are the consequences for us?

Has anyone expressed what happens to the sinner more eloquently than David? In a poem after his double failure: his adultery with Bathsheba and the murder of her husband, he wrote:

> When I did not confess my sins,
>     I was worn out from crying all day long.
> Day and night you punished me, LORD;
>     my strength was completely drained,

as moisture is dried up by the summer heat
                              (Psalm 32:3–4, GNB).

Commenting on another of the Psalmist's poems, Thomas Merton writes, 'A sinner is a drowning man, a sinking ship. The waters are bursting into him on all sides. He is falling apart under the pressure of the storm that has been breaking up his will, and now the waters rush into the hold and he is dragged down. They are closing over his head, and he cries out to God: "The waters are come in even unto my soul." The sinner is a person who knows his soul to be "logged with these icy waters".'[1]

Paul put it another way. To return to sin is to return to slavery. 'Freedom is what we have – Christ has set us free! Stand, then, as free people, and do not allow yourselves to become slaves again' (Galatians 5:1, GNB).

Those who do resort to sin's enslavement after their conversion to Christ face acute problems. As one young Christian expressed it, 'The more I get involved, the greater the pull seems to be. Then I search my soul and ask, "Do I really want to be different?" I find I'm so busy enjoying what is happening that I don't think about asking where it fits into the teaching of the Bible or what God has to say about it. I welcome and harbour wrong thoughts. I indulge in all kinds of fantasies.'

This man, though a Christian, had allowed Satan to weave a web around him once again. He was not free. He was hopelessly enslaved.

To encounter a person in this kind of bondage is one of the greatest tragedies of the Christian life. As we saw earlier, there is no need to return to this enfeebled state. Neither does God will it. We should see ourselves as part of the conquering army of Christ. Satan and his minions may yet lurk round every corner, but they have no power over us. We have power over them. With Christ we can drive them from our lives. But we have to be willing. We have to act as the mature, adult people Christ made us to be (see Galatians 5:13). We also have to recognize that our failure to defend our freedom affects the God whom we say we love.

## The effect of our sin on God

Sin stains. It stains our clean robe of righteousness with grime. It stains our consciences with guilt (see 1 John 3:4). It stains our reputation before God, even casting doubt on the efficacy of our conversion (1 John 3:7). And it separates us from the fellowship with God we once enjoyed. One Christian put the situation quite simply when he said: 'Sin is like slapping Jesus in the face. You see him hanging on the tree. You look at his dying form and say: "You died for me. You bore my sin. But I simply do not care."'

Jesus said, 'If you love me, keep my commandments.' Yet many of us today, who delight to be caught up in worship, singing, saying and even feeling, 'I love you Lord', 'I worship you', 'I adore you', walk out of the church door and sin blatantly.

Ezekiel shows us that the heart of God is torn when he perceives such inconsistency; when he is forced to watch a believer commit spiritual suicide: 'But if a righteous man stops doing good and starts doing all the evil, disgusting things that evil men do, will he go on living? No! None of the good he did will be remembered. He will die because of his unfaithfulness and his sins' (Ezekiel 18:24, GNB).

'"Do you think I enjoy seeing an evil man die?" asks the Sovereign LORD. "No, I would rather see him repent and live"' (Ezekiel 18:23, GNB).

The Old Testament is full of pictures which portray God's anguish as he contemplates man's wickedness, the anguish which tears his heart in two: the yearning to show mercy laced by the holiness which cannot coexist with evil.

Yet we Christians *say* we love God while deliberately plunging him afresh into this pain. We are inconsistent. The question, if we truly love God, if we are God-pleasers, is not, 'Do I want to change?' but 'How can I change?' In the face of God's unending, merciful, forgiving love, what *I* want simply doesn't come into consideration. I want what he wants. God tells us what he wants: our repentance, obedience.

### The way back: repentance

'"If an evil man stops sinning and keeps my laws, if he does what is right and good, he will not die; he will certainly live. All his sins will be forgiven, and he will live, because he did what is right. Do you think I enjoy seeing an evil man die? . . . No, I would rather see him repent and live"' (Ezekiel 81:21–23, GNB).

When we have disobeyed God there is a way back. The gateway is repentance.

Repentance means to face up honestly to the past and turn from it.[2]

Repentance turns us from sin, selfishness, darkness, idols, habits, bondages, and demons both private and public. We turn from all that binds us and oppresses us and others, from all the violence and evil in which we are so competent, from all the false worship that has controlled and corrupted us. Ultimately, repentance is turning from the powers of death. These ominous forces no longer hold us in their grip; they no longer have the last word . . . Repentance is seeing our sin and turning from it.[3]

But repentance is not purely negative, a turning from. Repentance is positive, a turning towards. Repentance is a re-orientation, a *metanoia*, the New Testament word for a complete and utter change, a chain of choices, an act of the will. Repentance is deliberately placing every part of our being – body, mind, imagination, talents, friendships, emotions, intellect, time – at God's disposal so that every part of our being becomes a weapon fighting for the holy war *against* sin. The repentant sinner flatly refuses to wage war on the side of sin.

The repentant person is a humble person. He is unafraid to request a special empowering of the Holy Spirit to enable him to conquer known temptations. He is unafraid to give God access to the hurts which prevent him from obeying. He allows the Holy Spirit to permeate even the hidden recesses of his intellect, emotions and psyche so that he becomes truly God's man, truly free.

## A dedication of the will

Repentance may or may not be accompanied by

remorse. Again Christians are divided into two camps. Some, when they become aware of sin in their lives, become guilt-stricken, oppressed, sorrow-laden. They confess until their knees are sore with praying but they fail to enjoy forgiveness. Others grow cynical, bitter, sin-hardened. 'God knows what I'm like. He saw the temptation coming. So why didn't he prevent me from falling?'

To both sets of Christians it must be said that in this area of our lives feelings must not be allowed to predominate.

By all means give vent to your sorrow. David did. Weep the tears of repentance. They are therapy. Let out the stale air of sin-orientation. Let the Holy Spirit's conviction pierce you like a knife. But do not stay with these feelings. You must focus, not so much on your sin, as on the sin-bearer, Jesus. Allow him the privilege of wiping your eyes dry. Allow him the joy of breathing into you the cool, clean air of forgiveness. Allow him to clean the festering wound, to heal over the incision made by the surgeon's scalpel. When we do not allow this healing, cleansing, forgiving ministry of Jesus, we fall into more sin: the pride which allows our sin to fill the horizon, obliterating the miracle of God's redeeming grace. Very often, to receive this forgiveness is an act of the will, a step of calculated faith.

## Rededication of the will

The sin-hardened Christian must also make a deliberate act of the will if he is to be restored. You may not *feel* guilty. You may heap all the blame on to God. You may blame others. The fact is that you are guilty.

Your guilt is punishable by God. You have turned your back on your resolve to live for God, to renounce 'sin, the world and the devil' as the Prayer Book puts it. The fact is that you have failed. The fact is that failure for the Christian is serious; to sin is to live a lie.

In his popular book, *Spiritual Depression*, Dr Martyn Lloyd-Jones urges us to be tough with ourselves when confronted with temptation, sin and the need to repent. He suggests that Christianity is far too often presented as a palliative:

> Come to the clinic and we'll give you all the loving care and attention that you need to help you with your problems.... In the Bible I find a barracks, not a hospital. It is not a doctor you need but a Sergeant-Major. Here we are on the parade ground slouching about. A doctor is no good; it is discipline we need. We need to listen to the Sergeant-Major – "Yield not to temptation but yield yourselves to God." This is the trouble with the Church today: there is too much of the hospital element: they have lost sight of the great battle.[1]

Some of us need to hear those strong words and take them to heart. Others *do* need a hospital. And as someone has rightly said, 'God prepares a hospital for those he has to wound.' Only *you* know which you need and by now I hope that you are learning to be really honest with yourself, with a self-awareness which prompts you to seek appropriate help from God.

Repentance, a rededication of the will and unstinting obedience to the will of God. These are the motors which propel us into true Christian freedom.

## Obedience: the way to freedom

Obedience is not an asset with which we are adorned at birth, it is an attitude of mind which is learnt. Even Jesus 'learned obedience from what he suffered' (Hebrews 5:8). This cannot mean that the perfect, sinless Son of God turned from disobedience to obedience. It must surely mean that Jesus learnt, through the bitterness of experience, that to obey the Father in the nitty-gritty of everyday life as a human being was costly, emotionally and sometimes physically.

This obedience asks God to cut it free from anything which is less than his best. This obedience is ever-ready, albeit with a struggle, to say yes to God – not one 'Yes', but a series of 'Yesses'. This obedience becomes an incarnation, 'A practical, daily aligning of our will with his'.[5] This obedience becomes an unconditional surrender. This obedience makes a profound effect on the believer, as André Louf points out:

> (Obedience) effects something in the one who obeys. It lays his life entirely open to the requirements of an Other and binds him fast to that Other. More, much more even than that. It can engender new life. By laying someone open to an Other, it alters him in the deepest sense of the word. It is a new life-style, whereby a person can detach himself more and more from his own constricted state, so as to be engrossed in the richness of an Other and to share that richness with Him.[6]

It follows that the repentant, dedicated, obedient Christian will not want to toy with sin. 'But you know that he appeared so that he might take away our sins. And in him is no sin. No-one who lives in him keeps on sinning' (1 John 3:5–6). Even so, such is the subtlety of Satan, there are some Christians who believe, as some of the early Christians seemed to do, that by the very act of their sin, they are ingratiating God; surrounding him with ever new opportunities to demonstrate his grace.

## Sin: pleasing to God?

Such a person was Colin. He was distraught when he recognized the emptiness of his own argument: 'I really have allowed my conscience to be lulled. I've been resting on a false sense of security – doing all the wrong things and thinking to myself, "Well, never mind. I can always confess them. God is forgiving. He'll take me back."'

Paul is scathing of such fallacious arguments. 'What shall we say, then? Shall we go on sinning, so that grace may increase? By no means! We died to sin; how can we live in it any longer?' (Romans 6:1–2). 'You, my brothers, were called to be free. But do not use your freedom to indulge the sinful nature' (Galatians 5:13). Moreover, the Bible seems to imply that whenever we Christians sin, we crucify Christ all over again (see Hebrews 6:6). Can we, then, deliberately sin without hearing the echo of the hammer resounding in our ears, without feeling the flesh of Christ flinch beneath the death-blow? It hurts to inflict pain on one you love. It should therefore hurt us when we deliberately sin.

The Christian free to sin? No way. The good news of the Christian gospel is that Christ has snapped the chains which once held us captive to sin. The good news is that we have gained a new word in our vocabulary. We are free – free to say a clear, resounding, unequivocal 'No' to the sin which, while we inhabit the overlap, lurks in the shadows to attack and destroy us. The good news is that we hold the trump card against sin. The good news is that we are free to serve, not sin, but God, whose service is perfect freedom.

## Notes for chapter ten

[1]Thomas Merton, *Meditations on the Liturgy* (Mowbrays, 1965), p.105.
[2]Jim Wallis, *Call to Conversion* (Lion, 1981), p.xiv.
[3]Jim Wallis, pp.4 and 5.
[4]D. Martyn Lloyd-Jones, quoted by D. Watson, *God's Freedom Fighters* (Movement Books, 1972), p.48.
[5]Maria Boulding, *Marked for Life* (SPCK, 1979).
[6]André Louf, *Teach Us To Pray* (Darton, Longman and Todd, 1978), p.28.

# 11

## *Free to serve*

When the lower nature, self, is freed, we are then free to serve.

Whole-hearted service is to the Christian what hot air is to the hot-air balloon: the vital fuel which keeps him airborne. Thus the Anglican Prayer Book claims that service of God is 'perfect freedom'. It is possible to receive God's healing in rich measure, it is possible to be rescued from failure by Christ's death, it is possible to be reinstated after a period of back-sliding, but unless you are prepared to serve you will never even begin to experience the Christian freedom for which you crave. His *service* is perfect freedom. You are saved to serve.

Isn't that a contradiction in terms? How can servitude become freedom? What is service? How do we go about it? What is group service? Is it possible to be overburdened with activities? Why can't I serve God more effectively?

These are the questions which will occupy our minds as this chapter unfolds.

## What is service?

Christian service, if we take Jesus' life as our example, does not originate in frenetic activity. Service, for Jesus, began with a relationship, continued with an attitude, and was expressed by availability. Specific acts of service were an off-shoot of a deep commitment.

### A relationship

What was it that enabled Jesus, of his own free will, to renounce the equality he shared with God and to assume instead the guise of a servant (see Philippians 2:7)? What was it that persuaded him to exchange the splendour of heaven for the crude exposure of the crib? What was it that pushed him to say yes to the cross of Calvary? It was love for the Father. In the vocabulary of Jesus, love and obedience are synonymous. What the Father asked, he did. His motivation was a deep, sustained and sustaining love. 'I have obeyed my Father's commands and remain in his love' (John 15:10). To the Christian, love, obedience and service mean one and the same. Christian service is loving God through loving others in any way God asks. Christian service is the grateful, open dedication of one's entire self to God. The Christian, conscious of the oppressive regime from which he has been rescued, voluntarily donates his all to the rescuer, God. It is as simple, as profound and as costly as that.

### An attitude

When the starting-point for service is the Father-heart of God there is only one attitude of mind which is open to us. Jesus is our pattern. In his own words, 'For even

172

the Son of Man did not come to be served, but to serve' (Mark 10:45). Submission to the Father expressed through a donation of all he had and all he was to men, one shade of submission's true meaning, was the life-principle selected by Jesus. The driving force of Paul's life was similar. He chose for himself the label, 'servant of Christ' (Romans 1:1; Philippians 1:1; Titus 1:1). A voluntary slave is one who has renounced all personal rights to ownership of possessions, decision-making, self-aggrandisement. A voluntary slave vows to spend his entire life serving his master in any way the master should request. Paul admonishes us to be similarly motivated. 'Let Christ Jesus be your example as to what your attitude should be. For he, who had always been God by nature, did not cling to his prerogatives as God's equal, but stripped himself of all privilege by consenting to be a slave . . . he humbled himself by living a life of utter obedience' (Philippians 2:5–8 Phillips). And, as we have already noted on more than one occasion, Jesus was totally and utterly free. It is another mystery. An intriguing paradox. We can be slaves, yet free.

*Free slaves*

True service begins with a relationship and it is kept in motion through acceptance: acceptance of our servant-hood. When we consent to be Christ's slave, when we humble ourselves under his almighty will, when we donate all that we have and all that we are to a life of utter obedience, a miracle takes place. We are set gloriously and exhilaratingly free.

You can prove this for yourself. You are tempted to disobey God in an area of your life which matters to you immensely. You are therefore confronted with a choice:

to go your way – or God's. You feel the full force of the struggle; the anguish of the cleft-stick. But then you take the leap of faith. You decide, albeit reluctantly, 'Not my way, Lord, but yours.' You expect to feel miserable. And what happens? Such joy floods your soul, such an awareness of God's love percolates through you, that you wonder why you ever paused at the cross-roads. No wonder Mary advised the servants, 'Do whatever he tells you' (John 2:5).

*Availability*

When our relationship with Jesus is governed by unashamed adoration and when this adoration expresses itself in the desire to have his mind in everything, we shall become totally available to him to be available to others as he directs. Availability is the kernel of Christ-like service.

Chris put this well when she reflected on her own Christian pilgrimage.

'When I first became a Christian, it was just like taking on another fascinating hobby. I added church-going, prayer and Bible-study to my other list of activities: badminton, swimming, singing, nursing.

'Then I got to know the Lord better and to love him more. One day he seemed to say to me, "It's not enough. I am not a hobby. I am Life." And I realized that to have Jesus as just another hobby *wasn't* enough. Jesus had to have all of me – or nothing. Christianity can't be just another hobby. Christianity is a whole way of life. Since I said to him, "OK, Lord. Take all of me," he's given me so many opportunities for serving him. It's funny. Now he's got all of me, I really feel fulfilled.'

Surely this was the attitude adopted by the early

disciples? Was this why they left an indelible mark on society from the Day of Pentecost onwards? Was this why they turned their world upside-down? Was this what lent persuasiveness to their claim that the Messiah had come? This was surely part of the reason for their effectiveness. In their willingness to serve they held nothing back. The person who clenches his fists around nothing holds out open hands – he is free.

## How do we serve?

The most effective way to serve God is to be the person he made you to be in the place where he wants you to be. As someone has expressed it, 'Grow where you are planted.' Or as someone else put it, 'A tree brings most glory to God by simply being a tree.'

There is a profound truth in those seemingly simple statements. Vicki helped me to see this when I was a patient in the hospital where she was on placement as a medical student.

When feelings of apprehension surfaced in me, Vicki was there: someone to listen, someone to pray with, someone who so evidently cared. When I was wheeled into the operating theatre, Vicki was there – grinning broadly, a grin which said, 'I'm praying.' When I came round from the anaesthetic, Vicki was there – still wearing her white coat, still smiling, her bright blue eyes saying, 'I'm glad you survived.' How did she manage to be so available? She sacrificed much-needed time off to be with me. Her presence was a ministry to me and a witness to the ward. Fellow-patients would ask me, 'Who is that young doctor?' And I would tell them, 'She's a member of our church.'

'Church' – to talk about Jesus after that was easy.

Very often Christian ministry is most effective when it takes place where we work. It is there we are asked to be Christ's representatives, his ambassadors. It is there we must live out his likeness.

Jim Wallis underlines the importance of this dimension of Christian service.

> When I was a university student, I was unsuccessfully evangelised by almost every Christian group on campus. My basic response to their preaching was, 'How can I believe when I look at the way the church lives?' They answered, 'Don't look at the church – look at Jesus.'
>
> I now believe that statement is one of the saddest in the history of the church. It puts Jesus on a pedestal apart from the people who name his name. Belief in him becomes an abstraction removed from any demonstration of its meaning to the world. Such thinking is a denial of what is most basic to the gospel: incarnation. People should be able to look at the way we live and begin to understand what the gospel is about. Our life must tell them who Jesus is and what he cares about.[1]

Taken on its own, this could be simplistic, but it does underline an important truth. This principle, incarnating the life and person of Jesus in my life, should be my primary goal; my life-ambition. It should also underscore every evangelistic project we adopt. People will be persuaded by our words about Jesus only when they are attracted by the Christ-likeness of our lives. That does not mean we should not speak for Christ until we are perfect. It does mean that we should acknowledge both sides of the coin of evangelism: forthrightness and sensitivity in speech; buying up every opportunity for God and the compelling attractiveness of a Christ-like life. It means that we acknowledge that Jesus drew men to the Father, not only because of what he said but because of who he was. It means that we begin to trust that, even if we are too shy to speak for Christ, yet in his great goodness he may be using the quality of our life as a tool for evangelism. It also means that we will lay at his feet all the good, all the talents, all the strengths that we are beginning to recognize within ourselves. It means that we will pray a prayer like this, 'Lord, use even me.'

## Lord, use even me

How might God use you?

One of the reasons why I have underlined the value of self-awareness and self-acceptance in this book is that these are crucial to dedicated service. Until you know who you are, what your gifts are, you cannot discover how you might most effectively make an impact for Christ in your corner of the world. You might even find others squeezing you into a mould which is not you-shaped at all; a mould which restricts your service for God rather than freeing you to serve. Be honest. Acknowledge your worth. Out of gratitude to God for his love for you, make an offering of yourself to him.

Maybe God has given you a love for children? That is a gift on trust from him. It can be used in helping with the crèche in your church, or in Sunday School teaching or baby-sitting.

Perhaps you are musical? Music is a gift God uses to

restore harmony to restless lives. Music soothes. God uses it to bring healing. Music can become a tool for evangelism. Music leads others into sensitive worship. Use your gift. The more you use it for God, the more it will be developed: and your spiritual life will be enriched.

Are you a friendly, hospitable person? Do you enjoy cooking? Hospitality is a ministry: use it, not just for entertaining friends but to draw in the needy, those searching for God; use it for outreach.

Perhaps you are a reflective person, not an activist, or perhaps you are no longer in a position to participate in the rush and tumble of life. Have you sought from God the gift of prayer? I thank God for the three women who pray for me every time I am counselling someone in need, even though they know nothing about the person or the need. I am indebted to the friends who undergird my ministry by praying for me daily whether they know what my schedule is or not. Mine is the up-front ministry; theirs is hidden. But who is to say which is of greater value in the economy of God?

I am not wanting to imply that God gives the gift of prayer only to the sick or the shy. Not at all. He gives this priceless gift of intercessory prayer to people of all ages and stages of Christian experience. Christians nation-wide are discovering that it is a powerful way to serve the church, the nation, the world. Intercessory prayer means coming alongside Jesus in his ongoing service of intercession, linking our prayer with his so that the power of God is unleashed for the persons or situations on our hearts. This powerful service must not be despised.

Do people come to you and pour out their problems?

Then maybe God has given you the gift of listening, a valuable gift God uses to bring consolation and healing to troubled hearts. Develop your gift by reading Myra Chave-Jones' outstanding little book, *The Gift of Helping* (IVP).

Can you read aloud well? Lesson-reading in church is a ministry. When someone reads with conviction, clarity and fluency, the Word of God goes forth with power and does its own work. This is a thrilling gift. If God has given it to you, use it.

Are you artistic? Has God given you the ability to communicate through photography, writing, collage, dance, drama? Thank God you live today. All of these can be channelled into serving him. When you relinquish your natural talents into the hand of God, inviting him to refine them, and then receive them back as custodian to use in his service, two things happen. First, you allow yourself to become a communicator of the good news of Christ, a faithful steward of the gospel (Luke 19:11–27). Second, although you may not recognize it yourself, you grow into ever-increasing freedom. This growth is characterized by an aliveness which attracts others so that your communication is double-edged: attractive and powerful.

## The group

The confidence to serve God often starts in small groups.

'Joyce, can you help me to discover my gifts? I don't seem to have any.' The speaker was Richard, a member of the youth club we were running. Richard and I tried to explore his strengths. He was right. There didn't seem to be many that were easily recognizable. He found the key for himself. 'About the only thing I'm good at is keeping things tidy.'

'Why don't you take on the job of tidying our lounge after the young people's meeting every Sunday? The place looks a shambles when everybody's gone: hymn-books, chorus sheets, coffee cups.'

Week after week, with no further invitation from me, Richard picked up the chorus sheets and left them in a neat pile. He organized others to wash the coffee cups. He stacked away the chairs and cushions.

I watched his confidence in himself and his sense of self-worth grow. Even so, some years later, when I re-visited the church, I could scarcely believe my eyes. Richard was running a youth group all on his own.

Service, like a beech tree, has a small beginning. We must not despise these small beginnings but see them for what they are: the seed which holds a life which will grow out of all proportion and beyond our wildest expectations. And we must beware of envying others the service God requires of them. Sometimes this will look far more exciting than any contribution we may make. Flamboyance is not the same as worth. Recognition is not the same as effectiveness. The service which pleases God is that which is conceived in devotion to him, which grows in the womb of our trust in him and which we offer to the world, sometimes with costly labour-pains, as a token of the inner prompting of love for Love. The group is the place where this growth is protected and from which it breaks forth. How?

When Len moved to a suburb of London, the church situation caused him near-despair. 'I went to one church after another. Nobody spoke to me. I'd heard about such things but never believed them. Now I know it's true. I travel into London every Sunday and in the middle of the week, just to get some fellowship. My job is tough enough without having a complete absence of Christian friends.'

When I asked Len what he appreciated about the group he attended, he smiled. 'There's a guy there with a real sense of humour. It's so good to laugh. I never laugh at work. Then there are a few who really take an interest in me. They seem to sense the strangeness and are helping me to settle in. There's one guy in particular. I'm beginning to feel I could share fairly deeply with him – and, what's just as important, he's beginning to share himself with me. Then there's the leader. He's only a young chap, but he's really good at leading Bible studies, and his wife – we meet in their home – is quiet but very hospitable. I'm beginning to see I'm very fortunate in being part of them.'

Float any one of those individuals in the fish-pond of the large church they attend each Sunday and they might be tempted to suspect that they can exercise no useful service for God. Here in the small group, each plays a vital part. When one person is missing, a vital ingredient is missing. The whole group is bereft.

Your role in your group might be to ensure, by your presence, that the group does not fossilize, nor become a doctrinal battle-ground. Every fellowship group should exist for three reasons: spiritual nourishment, people-making, and a purpose outside itself. If it is to fulfil its aims, it needs you together with the unique contribution only you can make. If relevant Bible-teaching is to feature, as it should, you may be the person to give it. If group members are to learn to share their worries, concerns and burdens with the group, it may be your sensitivity and spiritual discernment which is required to support them. If newcomers or the lonely are to be welcomed, your smile might be the ice-breaker. Shyness in groups is not a virtue but a withholding of your uniqueness which God needs for his own purposes.

But a group should never exist just for itself. A friend of mine said recently: 'Christian groups exist for others. Therefore join hands and face outwards.' Groups can become as self-centred and introverted as individuals. A successful group surveys the neighbourhood, looks to God, and asks, 'How do you want to use us here?' Then it obeys. Obedience might result in organizing an evangelistic supper party or a children's holiday mission. It might start further back than that and involve praying that God would pierce the lethargy of a middle-class suburban settlement.

## Is it possible to overwork?

If all of this: personal service, group service, sounds demanding, it is. But it is never too demanding unless we ourselves make it so. When Jesus promised, 'My yoke is easy, my burden is light,' he promised not to break our back or our marriage by over-involvement in Christian activities. As we saw at the beginning of this chapter, Christian service stems from a loving relationship with the source of protective love. It is not frenetic activity. Those of us who become over-burdened with Christian meetings and engagements do so because we are disobedient to the Lord's call, not because we are God's VIPs. As one friend of ours used to warn, 'If you are doing too much, you are doing more than the Lord intended.' Stop. Listen. Prune. Or, more accurately, allow the Lord to lop off the activity which should not be there because he has not required it of us. This is a discipline to which all Christians need to submit from time to time.

One quick, easy, infallible test of over-activity is this. Ask yourself how your prayer-life is going. If your response is, 'I'm too busy to pray,' then you are too busy. All service of God should originate in God and be soaked in prayer. If we are too busy to pray, we are too busy.

## Why am I not more effective?

Another test is this. Ask, 'Am I living biblically with regard to my wife, my husband, my children, my parents?' God does not want us to neglect our responsibilities for our loved ones by performing tasks in church work which others can do.

Just as it is possible to become swept up in a whirl of over-activity, so it is possible to become discouraged in Christian service. Often the reason for this discouragement is that we apply worldly criteria to our Christian work. The world says. 'You prove your worth by your success.' Jesus proved his worth by his death. Jesus does not tell us to succeed, he does tell us to strive for the sake of the kingdom of God.

That is not to say we should not look for success in our evangelism, our counselling, our calling. But it does mean that even if we do not see fruit for ourselves, we should continue to serve. This service should always be offered, not in our own strength, but with the enabling of the Holy Spirit. This means keeping short accounts with God, confessing sin quickly, as S. D. Gordon reminds us.

He tells the story of a sleepy village in Colorado which was dependent on seasonal rainfall for its water-supply. One day, some enterprising young men ran pipes from the village to the clear lake in the hills. The village then boasted a plentiful and pure supply of water.

One morning, however, the housewives turned on their taps to find, not gushing water, but spluttering drops – and then nothing. The men climbed the hill. The lake was as full as ever. There were no breaks in the pipe. They were mystified.

People began to move away from the now prosperous village. It began to resume its sleepy-hollow existence once more.

One day, an official of the town found a note on his door-step. It was badly written but it bore an important message. 'If you'll jes pull the plug out of the pipe about eight inches from the top you'll get all the water you want.'

They found the plug. It was not very big, but big enough to fill the pipe and cut off the water-supply. When the plug was pulled out, the water ran freely.

Just as the water in a large reservoir can be held back by a small obstruction in a pipe, so the Holy Spirit's energy can be clogged by our sin. Those who serve must keep the connecting pipes clear. Or, as S. D. Gordon puts it, 'Get out the thing that you know is hindering.'[2] Then we shall experience the freedom willing service brings in its wake.

**How does service spell freedom?**

I don't pretend to understand fully *how* it works, how service makes us free. What I do claim to understand is that it does work. I am watching it happen to Angus at the moment. He came into the church fellowship a rude, rebellious, off-hand problem child. Then someone discovered his gifts. 'Your gifts have a place in our fellowship,' Angus was assured. 'We need you.' At first it was difficult for any group to absorb him. His angularities isolated him. But slowly and surely he softened. That is not to say he became soft. He channelled all his many strengths, not into negativity, but into serving God. This service freed him from the need to rebel, from the need to hurt others. It set him free to be the talented, gifted, lovable person God had always intended he should become. This service set him free to become a man set apart for God.

The key word is commitment. Commit yourself to God-pleasing and you are released from the pull of self-pleasing. This introduces into your life a new purpose. The person who knows where he is going streamlines his activities, dispenses with the unnecessary, delights in essentials. He not only knows where he is going – he arrives. And our destination as Christians is ultimate, unadulterated freedom.

### Notes for chapter eleven

[1] Jim Wallis, *Call to Conversion* (Lion, 1981), p.108.
[2] S. D. Gordon, *Quiet Talks On Power* (Revell, no date), pp.41–43.

# 12

# *Free at last*

I was driving behind a Volkswagen 'Beetle' the other day. The sticker in the rear window read: 'When I grow up I'm going to be a Rolls Royce.'

In an absurd sort of way that sticker sums up all I've been trying to say in this book. The difference is that Christian hope is not false optimism; it is certainty.

John describes the future splendour which will be ours, 'Dear friends, now we are children of God, and what we will be has not yet been made known. But we know that, when he appears, we shall be like him, for we shall see him as he is' (1 John 3:2).

'When he appears.' When he appears we shall be free at last, free from every vestige of self, free from sin, free from temptation, free to be with him. And so we wait in glad anticipation. We grow into freedom wondering what fresh freedoms are to come. The world may scoff and scorn but they cannot quench the hope which burns in our hearts like a brave candle. We wait.

This waiting reminds me of a moving scene in Richard Attenborough's much acclaimed film, *Gandhi*.

The scene takes place at a remote railway station in India. The platform is studded with waiting Indians. As the train approaches, two British soldiers survey the crowd from their hill-top vantage-point. One asks the other: 'What are they doing? What are they waiting for?'

His colleague replies, 'I've no idea. All I know is they received a telegram a few days ago. On it were three words, "He is coming".'

The train snorted to a halt. A man alighted: a small, brown, middle-aged man dressed in white home-spun cloth – Gandhi. The crowds surged forward to greet him. Dark eyes lit up, weary faces smiled. And the soldiers mocked at the reverence showered on this insignificant-looking native. Why the excitement? Here was just another Indian, here today, gone tomorrow. Gone tomorrow? They were not to know that this charismatic figure would lead his country into freedom from British rule. The thought had never even crossed their minds.

Neither can the world concede that our telegram from heaven has arrived. 'I am coming soon' (Revelation 3:11). The world cannot detect the thrill which tingles through our body as we read the Lord's promise, 'I am making everything new!' (Revelation 21:5). The world cannot believe that when he comes we shall be free at last, glorified. Yet this is the theme which echoes round the book of Revelation. As we read this book we stand on the threshold of Paradise: the garden of freedom.

Has anyone captured the atmosphere better than C. S. Lewis as he concludes his famous Narnia tales?

The things that began to happen after that were so great and beautiful that I cannot write them. And for us this is the end of all the stories, and we can most truly say that they all lived happily ever after. But for them it was only the beginning of the real story. All their life in this world and all their adventures in Narnia had only been the cover and the title page: now at last they were beginning Chapter One of the Great Story which no one on earth has read: which goes on for ever: in which every chapter is better than the one before.[1]

In the book of Revelation, too, every chapter is more thrilling than the one before. If you thirst for a taste of freedom, read the book through at one sitting. It is both thirst-quenching, like drinking from a clear mountain spring in summer, and tantalizing, like the smell of coffee being ground. What is this mouth-watering freedom?

## Free to serve

We saw in chapter ten that to serve him is perfect freedom. Weariness, sin and human limitations siphon off the energy we need to serve God whole-heartedly this side of eternity. But in Paradise we shall be free: free to 'stand before God's throne and serve him day and night in his temple'. Ceaseless, tireless, unhindered service. That is our destiny. It will be our delight; the sort of delight happily married people take in making one another happy.

## Free to worship

Those who serve are those who worship (Revelation 7:9–12). Worship is the glove which fits the hand of service. In heaven we shall be free for both: 'And his

servants will worship him. They will see his face . . .'
(Revelation 22: 3–4, GNB).

It has been said of western Christians that so far we have learnt to worship God only from the neck upwards. In heaven we shall be caught up in ceaseless worship: worship expressed in music and movement.

> Day and night they never stop saying:
> > "Holy, holy, holy is the Lord God Almighty,
> > > who was, and is, and is to come."

Then I looked and heard the voice of many angels, numbering thousands upon thousands, and ten thousand times ten thousand. They encircled the throne and the living creatures and the elders. In a loud voice they sang:

> > "Worthy is the Lamb, who was slain,
> > > to receive power and wealth
> > > > and wisdom and strength
> > > > and honour and glory and praise!"

Then I heard every creature in heaven and on earth and under the earth and on the sea, and all that is in them, singing:

> "To him who sits on the throne and to the Lamb
> > be praise and honour and glory and power,
> > > for ever and ever!"

The four living creatures said, "Amen," and the elders fell down and worshipped (Revelation 4:8; 5:11–14).

One is tempted to say, 'Fantastic!' and to leave it at that. But there is more. In heaven we shall be free to celebrate. Heaven is a celebration: for us and for God.

## Free for intimacy

Zephaniah focuses on the festival of heaven. 'Do not fear; do not let your hands hang limp. The LORD your God is with you, he is mighty to save. He will take great delight in you, he will quiet you with his love, he will rejoice over you with singing' (Zephaniah 3:17).

Here in this world, God's felt presence is, at best, fleeting, intermittent, transitory. In heaven we shall be so free from the changes and chances, the sorrows and pains, the tears and grief of this earthly life, that we shall enjoy intimacy with God permanently; fellowship with God for ever and ever. We shall know, not with the eye of faith, but with our whole being, that we belong to God, that God belongs to us. The words from the Song will ring with truth. 'I am my Beloved's, and my Beloved is mine' (Song of Solomon 6:3, JB). We shall know what it means to be the Bride of Christ.

## Free from temptation, free from sin

On that longed-for day, Satan's defeat will be final (Revelation 20:10). On that great day, good and evil will no longer live cheek by jowl. Sin will be eradicated for ever. 'No longer will there be any curse' (Revelation 22:3). Sin will no longer pollute us. Sin will no more infect us. Sin will never hinder us again. The battles and struggles of earth will be over. The final battle will have been won. And we shall be radiant – his Bride.

I love the way Michael Wilcock introduces us to the Bride of Christ. Describing the New Jerusalem (Revelation 21:9–27), he writes,

We have passed beyond the bounds of space and time

into regions of eternal light, unshadowed by the slightest imperfection, not to say evil; where the eyes of every created thing are fixed in adoration upon the Lamb alone. *Yet he is not alone.* For sharing the Scene with him – indeed, taking its very title role – is a radiant stranger whose features, as we consider them, are nonetheless familiar. Can it be . . .?

It is 'the Bride, the wife of the Lamb'. It is the church of Christ. *It is you; it is I.* Whatever other metaphors we may use to describe our relationship with Christ, the last Scene of the Bible shows us ourselves married to him, 'cleansed . . . by the washing of water with the word', presented before him 'in splendour, without spot or wrinkle or any such thing' (Ephesians 5:26–27).[2]

Let us feast our minds on these truths. Let them peal through the churches like the bells of Bethlehem on Christmas morning. The magnetic quality of their exhilarating joy keeps us facing in the right direction: away from the slavery of sin, facing freedom.

And there we must leave the gateway of heaven, not to become earth-bound again, but to live life on this planet while determining that, as far as we are able, we will prepare ourselves for home: heaven. Freedom.

## Preparing for freedom

Prepare ourselves? The main thrust of this book has been to show that it is the Holy Spirit who prepares us for this privileged wifely role. That we may be presented to our heavenly bridegroom 'without spot or wrinkle or any such thing' his love is sometimes tough, as we have seen. Toughness is a greater sign of love than sentimentality. A silversmith in Greece demonstrated this to me once.

I was browsing in his shop, fingering his silver filigree work, when out of the corner of my eye I saw him. In his hands he held a pair of iron tongs, blackened with soot. He used them to remove a silver chalice from a shelf. I stared, indignant in my ignorance, as he thrust the chalice into the furnace which blazed at the back of the shop. He seemed to sense my dismay for when the time came to withdraw the chalice from the flames, he beckoned me to me. He grinned as, with a soft cloth, he wiped the chalice clean. And even my inexperienced eye could see the improvement. The silver, now refined, gleamed.

Life in the overlap is about refining. Refining precedes radiance. The heavenly silversmith knows how long to hold you in the crucible of his love. As soon as you are free of dross, there will be no more need for purging. You will be free.

Freedom in the overlap is, at best, restricted freedom. We are like butterflies testing our wings in a large auditorium. We are no longer caterpillars. We have multi-coloured wings. To fly is fun. But, from time to time, we press against the window-pane sensing that a greater freedom is only a pane of glass away. It is. He is coming. He is coming to give us life (see Revelation 2:10). He is coming to set us free. When he comes we shall be like him. We shall be 'Free Indeed'.

## Notes for chapter twelve

[1]C. S. Lewis, *The Last Battle* (Puffin, 1964), p. 165.
[2]Michael Wilcock, *I Saw Heaven Opened* (Inter-Varsity Press, 1975), p. 205.